Xmas 1989

To

John

with best wishes for Xmas
and most grateful thanks for the
kindness you give me
may God richly bless you
Lots of love Mother.

D1341979

HYMNS

and their

WRITERS

by
Jack Strahan

OCTOBER 1989
Published by
GOSPEL TRACT PUBLICATIONS
411 Hillington Road, Glasgow G52 4BL, Scotland

ISBN 0 948417 55 2

Copyright © 1989
GOSPEL TRACT PUBLICATIONS

Printed by
GOSPEL TRACT PUBLICATIONS
411 Hillington Road, Glasgow G52 4BL, Scotland

When at the first I took my pen in hand,
Thus for to write, I did not understand
That I at all should make a little book
In such a mode.

(John Bunyan)

Foreword

At the dawn of Creation, the book of Job declares, "the morning stars sang together and all the sons of God shouted for joy" (Job 38:7), and when the sun is about to set on man's civilization a great multitude in Heaven, as the voice of many waters and as the voice of mighty thunders, bursts with triumphant praise, "Alleluia; for the Lord God omnipotent reigneth" (Revelation 19:6). In between these outstanding events the Word of God is marked by the voice of praise for "Great is the LORD, and greatly to be praised" (Psalm 48:1). The psalmists and other persons of note have had their expressions of adoration recorded in the book of God and these have been the "song book" of the redeemed of numerous generations. Early in the history of the Church individuals began to compose hymns containing fundamental New Testament Truths and some of these find their place in our New Testament, e.g.

> "Great is the mystery of godliness; God was manifest in the flesh, justified in the Spirit, seen of angels, preached unto the Gentiles, believed on in the world, received up into glory" (1 Timothy 3:16).

The centuries that have followed have brought forth a constant stream of poetic verse, dealing with various themes, all giving praise, worship and honour to our Glorious Lord.

The present publication is a selection of well-known and many well-loved hymns and their writers and we have no doubt the readers will be intrigued by such interesting information. The articles were first of all contributed by brother Strahan to the magazine, *Assembly Testimony*—they quickly became the most popular in the magazine and we are delighted that our brother agreed to revise and enlarge them—they are now presented in book form and we are sure they will bring much joy and profit to many. I heartily commend the book and urge you to read it.

A. M. SALWAY GOODING
1989

Preface

In the Hebrew Psalter, the "title" or "superscription" of a psalm often indicates its authorship and circumstances of writing; some understanding of this background is helpful to the appreciation of the psalm. Likewise, it is so in hymnology and to this end this book is an attempt, in a small way, to fill in the background of some of the hymns that we sing. In these pages the reader will be introduced to a number of interesting hymn-writers of preceding generations; for some readers the experience will be but a meeting again with old acquaintances, for others there will be new introductions, but whether old or new, I pray that the hours spent with them will be to pleasure and to profit.

Of the multitude of hymns that exist to-day there is no end, but among them are some that bear the hallmark of Heaven. Such have been born in the sanctuary and often out of deep personal experience. Through successive generations they have ministered help to countless souls and their greatness remains undiminished with the passing of the years. These are hymns that will never die and a number of such appear once again within these pages.

There are fifty short studies in this book, and every hymn considered is by a different author. Each study contains a brief biographical sketch of the author, the circumstances of the writing of the hymn (where known), some of the hymn's associations and its main focal message. Of necessity a selection has had to be made and some readers may be disappointed that their favourite hymn has been omitted. Indeed, many dearly-loved hymns are absent from this collection; in some cases there was insufficient biographical detail of the writer to merit their inclusion, in other instances an equally well-loved hymn by the same author was considered instead.

The studies are arranged chronologically, commencing with the ancient hymn of David of three millennia ago; then follow a few hymns of the early Church age, but most hymns are of English origin and mainly the product of the eighteenth and nineteenth centuries. In this era, known as the golden age of English hymnology, great spiritual revivals swept throughout these islands; God raised up human instruments for the proclamation of His Word and in like manner raised up men and women to write hymns for His glory. These hymn-writers were sovereignly chosen and taken from every rank and walk in life. Their individual contribution varied widely, that of some was but the inspiration of a moment, that of others was the labour of a lifetime.

The material of this book first appeared in serial form throughout the 1980's in the magazine *Assembly Testimony* and with the generous and courteous permission of its editors and committee is now sent forth in this more permanent form. Most of the articles are essentially as first published; a few have been augmented, some have been rewritten, but the majority have received minor alteration only.

I do not claim the material herein presented to be entirely my own. I have pursued many lines of enquiry and have received help from many sources. To all I wish to express my indebtedness. My pursuits have taken me on many interesting trips across Ireland, Great Britain and beyond, to glean information at first hand, but most of the material presented has been taken from previously published works. A selected bibliography of the more useful literary helps is appended at the close of this book; from this list I wish to make special mention of Dr. John Julian's monumental *Dictionary of Hymnology* which has been foundational and indispensable in the study. Throughout I have sought to acknowledge these sources of help but, if inadvertently, any copyright has been infringed it is hoped that this apology on the author's part will be accepted.

I am all too conscious that this volume has many shortcomings; only for the invaluable help of others the shortcomings would have been more numerous. I wish, therefore, to express my gratitude to a number of people in particular.

—to all those who, by word or letter, have communicated their appreciation of the original articles in *Assembly Testimony* and encouraged the production of this more permanent record.

—to Brenda Cassidy, my secretary, who painstakingly over the years typed all the original articles and this final manuscript.

—to A. M. S. Gooding, my esteemed brother in the Lord and editor of *Assembly Testimony*, for writing an appropriate foreword.

—to Jim Flanigan, my brother beloved, for valuable assistance in correcting the proofs.

—to the staff of Gospel Tract Publications, Glasgow, for their co-operation, guidance and assistance in the publication of this book.

My best thanks, however, are to a faithful God who has enabled me by His grace to share in this labour of love. It is sent forth in His Name with the sincere desire that through it He will be magnified and many hearts blessed.

JACK STRAHAN
ENNISKILLEN
MAY 1989

"Galilee"

1. Free and exhilar-ant thine air, Thy hills so grand, thy sea so fair, Beau -ty be -yond com -pare.

Here was the lot of Naphthali, Home of the man who came to die, The Man of Gal - i - lee.

2. The morning choral wakes the day,
   The shades of night, they flee away,
   Welcome dawn's sunlight ray,
   The birds, they seem as if to sing
   In praise of Him who is the King,
   "The Man of Galilee".

3. With vigour new, men ply the soil,
   The fishermen, now ceased night's toil,
   Are counting out their spoil.
   But holier service did He rend,
   That lowly man whom God did send,
   "The Man of Galilee".

4. The sunlight shimmers o'er the lake,
   Its waters glint with flow and wake,
   Of heavenly blue partake.
   Once feet Divine trod on thy shore,
   What human loveliness He wore,
   "The Man of Galilee"!

5. Day now has sped, withdrawn its light,
   Long shadows darkened into night
   And stars now shining bright.
   On top thy hills, upon the sod,
   There knelt a man who too was God,
   "The Man of Galilee".

6. Such lakeside scenes to muse upon,
   Of Matthew, Mark and Luke and John,
   Let other thoughts begone.
   What lovelier portraits can I scan,
   Of One Divine, yet truly man,
   "The Man of Galilee"!

J.S.

Galilee

Like a beautifully-set sapphire stone, the deep blue waters of the Sea of Galilee nestle peacefully among rolling hills of ever-changing hue; Galilee has natural beauties which are unique.

Galilee, however, has been enriched and hallowed by fleeting, yet unforgettable, links with its Creator. There, God the Son, in the days of His flesh, made for a time His home and stooped to touch His own creation. Though "Lord of all" (Acts 10:36), He knelt to pray on its lonely hill-top and slept from weariness as He crossed its turbulent sea. The beauties of "the Man of Galilee" have eclipsed, for all time, the natural beauty of Galilee's delightful land and sea-scapes.

"The Man of Galilee" is portrayed for us in the Gospels; there a glorious four-fold portrait unfolds and is alluded to in this poem which was written one November morning in 1980 at Ginosar on the Galilean lake-shore.

Some eight years later the words were set to music by Leonard B. Mullan of Carnlough; the tune is called "Ginosar".

Daybreak over Sea of Galilee
(from Ginosar)

Contents

"The Lord's my Shepherd"

David, son of Jesse (11th Century B.C.)

Eastern shepherd with his flock.

The Lord's my Shepherd, I'll not want;
    He makes me down to lie
In pastures green; He leadeth me
    The quiet waters by.

My soul He doth restore again;
    And me to walk doth make
Within the paths of righteousness,
    E'en for His own name's sake.

Yea, though I walk in death's dark vale,
Yet will I fear none ill;
For Thou art with me; and Thy rod
And staff me comfort still.

My table Thou has furnishèd
In presence of my foes;
My head Thou dost with oil anoint
And my cup overflows.

Goodness and mercy all my life
Shall surely follow me;
And in God's house for evermore
My dwelling place shall be.

This is probably the best known of the metrical versions of Psalm 23. It is commonly called the Scottish version and has been given to us by Francis Rous (1579-1659). "The King of love my Shepherd is" is a later rendering of the psalm by Sir Henry Williams Baker (1821-1877) and is very popular with many congregations.

Our Bible, like the Palace Beautiful in Bunyan's *Pilgrim's Progress* has many rooms. It has its Archives stored with annals of history—the historical books of our Bible. It has its Study and herein we have the masterpieces of Paul, of Peter and of the other apostles. It has its Observatory where we join the prophets and seers as they focus on the events of the future. But it also has its little private Chapel for quiet meditation, an undisturbed sanctuary, and this sacred retreat is the Book of Psalms.

Approximately one half of the psalms in the Psalter were given to us by David—David, the shepherd-king—David, a man after God's own heart and yet, at the same time, "a man of like passions as we". What a place these psalms of David have had within the hearts of God's people throughout succeeding generations!—to be sung in Solomon's Temple by the temple choirs—to be carried into captivity and sung by the rivers of Babylon—to be sung in synagogues, sabbath after sabbath—to be on the lips of Jesus of Nazareth from childhood days till He expired on the cross—to be crooned by the shepherds, the vinedressers, the ploughmen and the reapers of Palestine as they accomplished their daily task—to be revered by Jews scattered on every continent of this world; by every sick bed and lonely couch, on every wedding day, through valleys and over rugged paths, they still remain sweet to the people of God.

Psalm 23 is probably the best known and sweetest of all the psalms of David. We do not know for certain the time nor the circumstances of its writing, but it is probable that David wrote it in the closing years of life, for the words bespeak a quiet confidence mellowed by the experience of years of trial. Even though David has long since left us, he still speaks in this lovely shepherd psalm.

> *The harp strings lie bruised and broken,*
> *The kingdom has gone to decay,*
> *The shepherd-king sleeps in Mount Zion*
> *Not far from the ancient gateway.*
> *But the sweet tender song of the shepherd*
> *Sings on through the wearisome years;*
> *The shepherd may sleep, but his message*
> *Still lives to dispel human fears.*

Psalm 23 is immortal. Placed as it is in the Psalter between Psalm 22 ("The cross of suffering") and Psalm 24 ("The hill of glory"), this lovely "song of rest" is the psalm of present wilderness experience. These three psalms, taken together, cover the "yesterday, today and tomorrow" of Christian experience—the "yesterday" of the cross which is past, the "tomorrow" of the glory which is yet future and the "today" of present pilgrimage.

David had started out on the pilgrimage of life as a shepherd. Those were the delightful days of youth; but then the pathway took some unexpected turnings. Life held many dark days for David; public life had had its disappointments, family life had brought its heartbreaks and private life its own bitterness. Yet through it all, there was something remaining, untouched by the changing circumstances of time, and it is of this "something" that David now confidently sings—of the Shepherd and His abiding presence.

What sweet repose this is for the heart! Wants are negated by the provision of the Shepherd; weariness is dispelled in the green pastures and by the waters of quietness; wanderings are corrected and the soul is restored. Fears are cancelled though the valley be ever so dark; there is royal bounty even in the enemies' land, and the pathway, though maybe winding and steep leads on to the house of the LORD, for the Shepherd knows the way.

This unfailing Companion through life of whom David sings is Jehovah and what infinite resources obtain with Him!—all the know-how for the pathway and all the supply as well. He is at the same time both Shepherd and Host—as Shepherd, David is one of His sheep—as Host, David is one of His guests, at His table in the wilderness now, and then in the house of the LORD for ever.

A precious intimacy pervades the psalm, the intimacy of the Shepherd and His sheep. No stranger intrudes here. David feels his had been the privilege in life to have had Jehovah as his Shepherd and he now bears testimony to the greatness of His care. At the beginning of the psalm he speaks of the Shepherd as "**He**" (third person), but further on he addresses Him directly as "**Thou**" (second person). How sweet is this increasing intimacy! In the green pastures and by the still waters and in the paths of righteousness it is enough for David to speak of the Shepherd as "**He**", but as the road winds on through the dark valley and the enemies' land, it seems as if David moves closer to his Shepherd-guide and whispers to Him, "**Thou**". It is exceedingly precious for the child of God to be able to speak directly and intimately to the Shepherd when the sky darkens and the enemy is near!

Right at the outset of the psalm David lets us into the secret of all his blessings; it is this—"the LORD is my Shepherd". Everything else stems from this personal relationship. David here speaks of the Shepherd as, "my Shepherd". In John 10, the Shepherd speaks of the sheep as "my sheep". Such are the intimate relationships between the Lord and His own, so beautifully expressed in the words of the bride in the Song, "My beloved is mine, and I am his" (S.o.S. 2:16).

This psalm is a priceless heritage. By it steps are guided, tears are dried, the gloom is illuminated, fears are dissipated and dearest hopes revived. Dr. John Julian says of it, "the first religious verse learned at a mother's knee, and often the last repeated before entering the valley of the shadow of death".

"Art thou weary, art thou languid"

Stephen the Sabaite (725-794)
John M. Neale (1818-1866)

Monastery of Mar Saba.

Art thou weary, art thou languid,
  Art thou sore distress'd?
"Come to Me", saith One, "and, coming,
  Be at rest!"

Hath He marks to lead me to Him,
  If He be my guide?
In His feet and hands are wound prints,
  And His side!

Hath He diadem as Monarch
  That His brow adorns?
Yea, a crown in very surety,
  But of thorns!

If I find Him, if I follow,
  What His guerdon here?
Many a sorrow, many a labour,
  Many a tear!

If I still hold closely to Him,
  What hath He at last?
Sorrow vanquished, labour ended,
  Jordan pass'd!

If I ask Him to receive me,
  Will He say me nay?
Not till earth and not till heaven
  Pass away!

Finding, following, keeping, struggling
  Is He sure to bless?
Saints, apostles, prophets, martyrs,
  Answer, "Yes!".

The most fine gold is hidden deep in the earth, silently awaiting the coming of the workman to bring it to the surface and extract it from the ore. So, throughout long centuries some of the most precious treasure in hymnology lay buried deep, awaiting the coming translator. The Latin and Greek monasteries both held precious store. Then in the 19th century, two master workmen in these fields arrived on the scene. Edward Caswell extracted much precious treasure of the Bernards from the Latin mines, while John Mason Neale descended the hitherto unexploited Greek mines and retrieved for us some of the finest gold in hymnology.

In the early Christian era, the persecution of believers in the Lord Jesus was very real and many laid down their lives in martyrdom. As the tide of Mohammedanism swept through the Middle East (Jerusalem fell in 636 A.D.) and the then-known world, Christians were driven to take refuge. John of Damascus, who had held high office in his native city under a Moslem Caliph abandoned everything and taking with him his ten year old nephew Stephen, went into voluntary exile, secluding himself for the remainder of his life in the very ancient Greek monastery of Mar Saba.

Mar Saba lies half a day's journey from Jerusalem in "one of the most stricken wildernesses of the world", where the Kidron breaks through the "horrible abysses" of the scarred and furrowed Judean hills on its way to the Dead Sea. The monastery is best approached today by trekking eastward from Bethlehem over the waste rolling Judean wilderness. It is an intriguing but ghostly spot, so lonely and so remote that the heart is appalled at its desolation. The monastery itself, founded by St. Saba in the 5th century, is perched high on the face of the precipice of the Wady-en-Nar. From the tower of the monastery to the bottom of the defile where the Kidron threads its way, is a sheer drop of one thousand feet. Thus, like an eagle's nest, clinging perilously to the tawny rock, this most ancient religious institution has defied the ravages of time and the wars of men for fifteen hundred years. It is still inhabited today by a few monks of the present Greek Orthodox Church and housed within its walls are telling evidences of its very remarkable past—its "sepulchre of St. Saba" exhibits the mummified body of its founder hero of the 5th century, while its "chamber of the skulls" declares the fidelity to martyrdom of some fourteen hundred of its monks.

Mar Saba, in her past, has sheltered in times of persecution some of the choicest saints of the early Christian Church and out of her have come some of the most beautiful Christian hymns. In the 7th, 8th and 9th centuries, when religious strife was loudest in the world without, there arose within these monastic walls a remarkable group of poetic men. Among them the foremost were John of Damascus and his nephew Stephen. Stephen lived in the seclusion of Mar Saba for some sixty years until his death in 794 A.D. and this long association with St. Saba's institution earned for him the title, "Stephen the Sabaite". It is heart-thrilling to remember that the strains of Stephen's original Greek hymn were first raised on the ramparts of that ancient monastery. It would seem as if the limitations of his earthly horizons brought the heavenly very near.

The hymn, as we know it in English today had, however, to

await the coming of John Mason Neale in the 19th century. Neale was a man of literary genius and a poet besides. He was born at Conduit Street, London, on January 24th, 1818. After his early studies at Sherborne Grammar School, he entered Trinity College Cambridge in 1836. His career there was brilliant and he was reckoned the finest classical scholar of his period. He mastered some twelve languages and had a good knowledge of eight others.

Following graduation in 1840, Neale's ill health necessitated his temporary retirement to Madeira for a period and on his return to England he settled in Sussex as Warden of Sackville College in East Grinstead. Though termed a college, this was nothing other than an alms-house, an institute for the poor, a home for the aged. John Mason Neale, with all his outstanding literary capabilities, elected to spend the remaining twenty years of his life in that institution caring for the under-privileged and all for the meagre monetary reward of twenty-seven pounds per annum. Neale's years at Sackville College, however, were not wasted but fully occupied in diligent literary pursuits and proved very fruitful. Untiringly, day by day, he was extracting the finest of the gold from Oriental hymnology. As a consequence, he published in 1862 his *Hymns of the Eastern Church*. His *Collected Hymns* followed later and were published after his death.

John Mason Neale, through his labours, brought much to light from the libraries and monasteries of the Continent and the East and is esteemed as "the most distinguished and successful of all the translators". His literary skill was linked with a deep personal humility and matched by courage and dedication. In the face of ill-health and much opposition he carried on his task, and the final gold he cast unreservedly into the treasury of his Lord. His translations were with a master hand. Most were faithful to the original Greek but some were free (not so much an accurate translation of the text but rather a paraphrasing or adaptation thereof). Such is his hymn, "Art thou weary, art thou languid". Though the original of "Stephen the Sabaite" has been greatly modified the truth and spirit of the hymn have been preserved. Indeed, Neale's modification has added to the beauty and impressiveness of the hymn.

In English, the hymn first appeared in 1862 in Neale's *Hymns of the Eastern Church* (First Ed.) and was entitled "Rest in Jesus". It consists of seven stanzas, each of which is composed of a question and an answer. Each question is pertinent and the answer direct and explicit. The hymn is very personal and intimate; it is the essence of simplicity and beauty. The focus is on the Saviour throughout—His person is unmistakable, His pathway undeceiving, and His promise unfailing.

> *If I ask Him to receive me,*
>   *Will He say me nay?*
> *Not till earth and not till heaven*
>   *Pass away!*

"Jesus, the very thought of Thee"

Bernard of Clairvaux (1091-1153)

Bernard of Clairvaux.

The Dark Ages were still casting their shadow over Europe when Tesselin, a medieval knight who had fought in the First Crusade, returned to his castle on Les Fontaines near Dijon in Burgundy and there he joined his wife, the Lady Aletta. To this noble couple a son was born in the year 1091; they called him Bernard. Possessed of every favour and advantage—of high birth, of personal beauty, of gentle manner, influential and well educated, this world held great promise for Bernard. Lady Aletta, however, had loftier ambitions for her boy; she prayed for him and desired that he would be "a saintly messenger of God" and, though she didn't live to see her prayers answered, she died in faith. Bernard, at that time, was just fourteen.

At the age of twenty-two Bernard entered monastic life in the Cistercian Monastery of Cîteaux near Dijon. Such was his strength of personality and powers of influence that, on entering monastic life, he persuaded an uncle and two brothers to join him. Within the Cîteaux Order the ascetic practices were extremely stringent; however, Bernard observed them with diligence, even at times to the extent of endangering his health. Within the monastery, Bernard's austerity and perseverance brought him great admiration and early promotion.

After two years Bernard was sent forth from Cîteaux as leader of a group of twelve monks to found a daughter institution. Locating a spot in the pathless forest of the "Valley of Wormwood", they set to work amid great privations. The site was cleared, transformed, and a monastery was established; they called it "Clairvaux".

Bernard was abbot in the monastery at Clairvaux. He had, besides, the mind of a statesman and his fame quickly spread throughout Europe. His extraordinary influence and leadership involved him with kings, emperors and popes. His reputation for saintliness was such that people came from all parts to seek his guidance. Martin Luther, centuries later, testified of him, "If there ever lived on earth a God-fearing and holy monk, it was Bernard of Clairvaux".

Though Bernard travelled widely throughout Europe and beyond, his happiest days were spent within the monastery at Clairvaux. There he enjoyed sweet communion with God and there he committed many of his meditations to writing. At Clairvaux he spent the closing days of his life and there he passed away on August 10th, 1153, in his sixty-third year. His closing words, "I am no longer of this world", suggest that he was weary of this empty passing world and glad to be at rest.

Bernard of Clairvaux was a man of extraordinary talent and scholarship, an eloquent preacher of the gospel and a theologian of rare literary ability. His contribution to hymnology was significant and mainly in the form of Latin poems. The two best known which have been preserved to us are "Jesu dulcis memoria"—a poem on the name of Christ, and "Jesu mundi Salutare"—a meditation on the suffering Saviour. The latter consisted of three hundred and fifty lines and was divided into seven parts. The seventh part, on the suffering face of the Lord Jesus, was translated into German by Paul Gerhardt over five hundred years later, and from the German there have been several English translations, of which perhaps the best known is the very beautiful rendering by Dr. J. W. Alexander, "O sacred head, once wounded".

Bernard's other poem, "Jesu dulcis memoria" has been termed by Dr. Scaff, "the sweetest and most evangelical hymn of the Middle Ages". Some have expressed doubt as to whether Bernard did write this poem, but the best authorities are satisfied that it came out of the monastery at Clairvaux and that Bernard must have been its author. In its Latin original, the poem consisted of forty-two stanzas, of four lines each. David Livingstone tells us in his journals how he crooned it to himself in the wilds of Africa, "That hymn of St. Bernard on the name of Christ, although in what might be termed dog-Latin, pleases me so; it rings in my ears as I wander across this wild, wild wilderness".

There have been several complete and some partial translations of Bernard's poem and three of the most beautiful hymns in our English language have been derived from it:
  (1) "Jesus, the very thought of Thee" by Edward Caswell (1814-1878);
  (2) "Jesus, Thou Joy of loving hearts" by Ray Palmer (1808-1887);
  (3) "Jesus! The very thought is sweet" by John Mason Neale (1818-1866).

(1) *Jesus, the very thought of Thee*
        With sweetness fills my breast;
      But sweeter far Thy face to see,
        And in Thy presence rest.

   Nor voice can sing, nor heart can frame
     Nor can the memory find
   A sweeter sound than Thy blest Name,
     O Saviour of mankind!

(tr. by Edward Caswell)

(2) *Jesus, Thou Joy of loving hearts,*
     Thou Fount of life, Thou Light of men,
  From the best bliss that earth imparts
     We turn unfilled to Thee again.

  We taste Thee, O Thou living Bread,
     And long to feast upon Thee still;
  We drink of Thee, the fountain-head,
     And thirst our souls from Thee to fill.

               (tr. by Ray Palmer)

(3) *Jesus! The very thought is sweet,*
     In that dear Name all heart-joys meet;
  But sweeter than the honey far
     The glimpses of His presence are.

  No word is sung more sweet than this,
     No name is heard more full of bliss,
  No thought brings sweeter comfort nigh
     Than Jesus, Son of God most high.

          (tr. by John Mason Neale)

The person of Christ had filled and satisfied the heart of Bernard in the dark Middle Ages within the monastery at Clairvaux. Again and again, with soul athirst, he had turned aside from earth's best bliss to seek communion with Christ. Oft he had withdrawn from the oppression of sin's dark night, to rest in the light and warmth of the Saviour's presence. And still today the person of Christ is enough for the hearts of men. There is a sweetness in Christ for those that are tired of earth's tasteless fare; there is a kindness with Christ known and cherished best by those who have fallen, and with Him there is a fullness, an overflowing fount when other streams are dry.

"Commit thou all thy griefs"

Paul Gerhardt (1607-1676)

Paul Gerhardt.

A wealth of spiritual richness, probably surpassing all other, has been left for us by German hymn-writers; hundreds of men and women of all ranks contributed to this treasury of German song. The Reformation period was dominated by Luther with his hymns of clarity, strength and simplicity. The Post-Reformation period was enriched by the works of Gerhardt, Tersteegan and Zinzendorf.

Some of our greatest hymns have been born out of life's darkest experiences; the heart that is pressed and crushed often yields the sweetest music. It was so in the life of Paul Gerhardt; the fearful devastations and the horrible miseries of the Thirty Years War in Post-Reformation Germany together with deep personal sufferings, deprivations and misfortunes pressed from his heart some of our finest treasure in verse.

Paul Gerhardt, son of Christian Gerhardt, was born at Gräfenhaynichen near Wittenberg in Electoral Saxony on March 12th, 1607. Little is known of his early life during the period of the Thirty Years War, when Germany was torn in religious rivalry but it is generally believed that such troublesome times accounted for his late settlement, at the age of forty-four, in the ministry of the Lutheran Church.

Gerhardt entered his first pastorate in Mittenwalde and remained there about five years. He then moved to Berlin where he anticipated a happy ministry, but it was there that his greatest trials awaited him. Though a peace-loving man, he found himself inextricably entangled in the animosity and strife between the Lutheran and the Reformed Churches. His liberty was curtailed in the pulpit; he was crippled in his ministry and finally was pressed upon to sign the Elector's edict. Conscience, however, restrained him and he was deposed from office. Thus deprived of means of sustenance, he was much cast upon God.

At this particular time family trials weighed heavily. Having been bereft of four of his five children there now rested upon him the burden of a sick wife under very straitened circumstances; soon she too passed away. Then, as a widower with one remaining child, Gerhardt moved back to his native Saxony and at Lübben spent the closing seven years of his ministry. Very little is recorded of those years but we know that be died at Lübben on June 7th, 1676, in his seventieth year, and that he passed away from this world of trial and strife with the words of one of his own hymns upon his lips:

> Death can never kill us even,
> But relief
> From all grief
> To us then is given.
> It doth close life's mournful story,
> Makes a way
> That we may
> Pass to heav'nly glory.

He was buried in the church at Lübben. A portrait in oils marks the spot and underneath it the inscription (in Latin), "A theologian experienced in the sieve of Satan"; following this is a short epigram by Wersdorf:

A graven, indeed, yet living image of Paul Gerhardt,
In whose mouth, faith, hope, love have ever been.
Here Asaph returned to life, taught in our coasts,
And sang Thy praises, O gracious Saviour.

Paul Gerhardt has left for us a rich legacy in his spiritual songs. These number well over one hundred and of their worth Wackernagel writes, "High and low, poor and rich alike, find them equally consoling, equally edifying; in all stations, among young and old, there are examples to be found where some song of Gerhardt at particular periods in the history of the inner life was engraven forever on the soul . . . Gerhardt's hymns have quickened many hearts in heavy affliction and anxiety, and have quietly composed their minds in the hour of death and led them to peace".

Paul Gerhardt is indeed "the prince of German hymnists of the 17th century". "After Luther, I know no better hymn-poet than Gerhardt", says T. F. Hippel, "A certain impressiveness, a certain sorrowfulness, a certain fervour, were peculiar to him; he was a guest on earth . . . The songs of no other poet, either before or since, have ever produced so mighty an effect".

A considerable number of Gerhardt's hymns have been translated from the German and included in some form or other in our English hymn books. One of Gerhardt's finest hymns is "Befiehl du deine Wege" ("Commit thou all thy griefs"). It is based on Psalm 37:5 and was written during a very dark period of his life.

The following account is given of the circumstances surrounding its writing. "Having no certain dwelling place, he set out with his wife and family to return to his fatherland, Electoral Saxony. One evening while putting up in a Saxon village, his wife became very downcast, bemoaning their hard lot. Gerhardt tried to comfort her by reading Psalm 37:5, 'Commit thy way unto the LORD; trust also in Him; and He shall bring it to pass'. The truth of the words, though failing to bring peace to her, so impressed his own heart that he sat down and straightway wrote out the hymn, 'Befiehl du deine Wege'. He then came and read it to his wife and she was immediately comforted. Later that same evening, the messengers of the Duke of Saxe-Merseberg arrived bearing a letter to Gerhardt with promise of provision to meet his temporal need".

There have been many translations of this hymn into English but perhaps the most beautiful is that by John Wesley.

> Commit thou all thy griefs*
>   And ways into His hands,
> To His sure truth and tender care,
>   Who heaven and earth commands.
>
> No profit canst thou gain
>   By self-consuming care:
> To Him commend thy cause; His ear
>   Attends the softest prayer.
>
> Thy everlasting truth,
>   Father, Thy ceaseless love,
> Sees all Thy children's wants, and knows
>   What best for each will prove.
>
> Give to the winds thy fears;
>   Hope, and be undismayed,
> God hears thy sighs and counts thy tears,
>   God shall lift up thy head.
>
> Though years and years roll on,
>   His covenant shall endure;
> Though clouds and darkness hide His path,
>   His promised grace is sure.
>
> Through waves, and clouds, and storms
>   He gently clears thy way;
> Wait thou His time; so shall this night
>   Soon end in joyous day.
>
> Leave to His sovereign sway
>   To choose and to command;
> So shalt thou, wondering, own His way
>   How wise, how strong His hand.

In some hymnals this hymn commences, "Put thou thy trust in God".

These lines have been judged by Lauxmann, "The most comforting of all the hymns that have resounded on Paul Gerhardt's golden lyre, sweeter to many souls than honey and the honey-comb . . . truly a hymn surrounded by a cloud of witnesses". Its words are meaningful and strengthening, especially to the soul whose sky is dark and path untraceable. God is sovereign in all His ways, yet ever wise and kind; His sufficiency for every circumstance in life invites an unquestioning trust, then afterward begets an adoring wonder.

"Praise God from Whom all blessings flow"

Thomas Ken (1637-1711)

Thomas Ken.

Praise God from whom all blessings flow;
Praise Him, all creatures here below;
Praise Him above, ye heavenly host,
Praise, Father, Son, and Holy Ghost.

This immortal doxology was penned by Thomas Ken, and has probably been sung more frequently than any other stanza in hymnology over the past three hundred years. However, these words were not originally written as a separate doxology but at first appeared as the concluding verse of three of Thomas Ken's hymns—his morning hymn, "Awake my soul, and with the sun", his evening hymn, "All praise to Thee, my God, this night", and his midnight hymn, "Lord, now my sleep does me forsake".

Thomas Ken was born at Berkhampstead, Hertfordshire, England, in July, 1637. His mother who was the daughter of a poet died when Thomas was only five. His father died when he was fourteen and young Thomas then came under the care of an older married sister, Ann, and her devout and gentle husband, Isaac Walton. Walton, a very distinguished angler, had a refining influence on young Thomas and many hours they spent together by the river bank.

Thomas was educated at Winchester School and later at Oxford where he graduated B.A. in 1661 and M.A. in 1664. He was ordained in 1662 and following ordination served as chaplain to the Bishop of Winchester.

The years that followed were some of the most momentous in English history and Ken's ecclesiastical career was deeply affected by the rapidly changing events. In 1679, he was appointed as chaplain to Princess Mary and this took him to the Royal Court at the Hague in Holland. There, in that court, he witnessed immorality; he openly denounced it and this led to his dismissal. He returned to Winchester and in 1684 was appointed chaplain to King Charles II. When, at Winchester, the king sought the use of Ken's residence as quarters for his mistress, Ken bluntly and resolutely refused. He would not consent to the king's request; "No, not for the king's kingdom". The king in return esteemed Ken highly for his manliness and integrity and advanced him to the bishopric of Bath and Wells. A few days afterwards Ken was summoned to minister at the king's death-bed and this he did solemnly and faithfully.

Ken swore allegiance to the new monarch, King James II, but three years later incurred the king's wrath by refusing to comply with the reading of the Royal Declaration of Indulgence. He was not "afraid of the king's commandment". However, for this misdemeanour, he was committed to prison in the Tower of London, there to await trial, but at the end he was triumphantly acquitted.

Three years later when William III came to the throne, Ken, strong Protestant though he was, felt that he could not in all good conscience take the oath of allegiance to the new king while King James II was still alive, though in exile. Ken, therefore, was deprived of his see. "With his lame horse, his famous flute, his little Greek testament and his shroud", he took leave of his friends and the palace and went to live at Longleat, the home of an old college friend, Viscount Weymouth, and there he spent the last twenty years of his life.

> Dead to all else, alive to God alone,
> Ken, the confessor meek, abandons power,
> Palace and mitre, and cathedral throne,
> (A shroud alone reserved,) and in the bower
> Of meditation hallows every hour.

Increasing communion with God marked those closing years of Ken's earthly pilgrimage and the shaded groves around that princely retreat at Longleat on the Somerset/Wiltshire border were often made vocal with his morning and evening hymns.

> I, the small dolorous remnant of my days,
> Devote to hymn my great Redeemer's praise;
> Aye, nearer as I draw towards the heavenly rest,
> The more I love the employment of the blest.

Ken died at Longleat on March 19th, 1711, at the age of seventy-three and was laid to rest "at the rising of the sun" aside the eastern window in the parish church of Frome. The company, gathered for his simple funeral service, united together in singing the words of his lovely morning hymn.

> Awake my soul, and with the sun,
> The daily course of duty run;
> Shake off dull sloth, and early rise,
> To pay thy morning sacrifice.
>
> Redeem thy mis-spent time that's past
> And live this day, as if thy last;
> Improve thy talent with due care,
> For the great Day thyself prepare.

Let all thy converse be sincere,
Thy conscience as the noon-day clear;
Think how all-seeing God thy ways
And all thy secret thoughts surveys.

Awake, lift up thyself, my heart,
And with the angels bear thy part,
Who all night long unwearied sing,
Glory to the eternal King.

Praise God, from whom all blessings flow,
Praise Him all creatures here below,
Praise Him above, ye heavenly host
Praise Father, Son, and Holy Ghost.

Ken was a man of exceptional character. His whole life was one paean of praise to God. The letters he wrote were usually headed, "All glory be to God". His last recorded words were the same. H. L. Bennett in his tribute says, "The saintliness of Ken's character, his combination of boldness, gentleness, modesty and love, have been universally recognised". He was filled with the love of Christ and constantly left behind him a fragrance wherever he went.

Though Ken never married, he was very fond of children and it was to the boys of Winchester School that he gave his three great hymns. A Manual of Praise for the Use of the Scholars of Winchester College was published in 1674 and in this Ken enjoined the boys of the college, "Be sure to sing the morning and evening hymn in your chamber devoutly, remembering that the psalmist, upon happy experience, assures you that it is a good thing to tell of the loving-kindness of the Lord early in the morning and of His truth in the night season".

Ken used these hymns regularly in his own personal devotions, morning and evening, right to the close of life. He had a beautiful voice and sang them to the accompaniment of the viol or spinet, and was accustomed to remark that it would enhance his joy in Heaven to listen to the morning and evening hymns as sung by the faithful on earth.

And should the well-meant song I leave behind,
With Jesus' lovers some acceptance find,
'Twill heighten even the joys of heaven to know
That, in my verse, saints sing God's praise below.

The familiar stanza, completing each of Ken's three great hymns, is truly a wonderful doxology. No hymn book is complete without it. It has been the death song of martyrs and the paean of victorious armies. It was sung with great effect at Queen Victoria's Diamond Jubilee service by ten thousand people in front of St. Paul's Cathedral, and no matter where the people of God are assembled and a spirit of gratitude fills their hearts, it is wont to find expression in the words of Ken's doxology. Indeed, in the experience of the child of God, the lines of Ken's doxology seem to become increasingly meaningful with the passing of the years of life. James Montgomery says of it, "It is a masterpiece at once of amplification and compression, amplification on the burden 'Praise God', repeated in each line; compression by exhibiting God as the object of praise in every view in which we can imagine praise due to Him; praise for all His blessings, yea, for all blessings, none coming from any other source—praise, by every creature, specifically invoked, 'here below' and in Heaven 'above'; praise to Him in each of the characters wherein He has revealed Himself in His Word, 'Father, Son, and Holy Ghost' ".

Ken's doxology is a call to every living creature to praise God, the great Benefactor of all. In its original, it formed the great climax and conclusion of his morning, evening and midnight hymns; verses which were at once an exhortation and a prayer culminated in a final call to the exercise of praise. The great Psalter in our Bible culminates and concludes in a similar theme, "Let everything that hath breath praise the LORD. Praise ye the LORD" (Psalm 150:6).

> *Praise God from whom all blessings flow,*
> *Praise Him, all creatures here below;*
> *Praise Him above, ye heavenly host;*
> *Praise Father, Son, and Holy Ghost.*

"When I survey the wondrous Cross"

Isaac Watts (1674-1748)

Isaac Watts.

As the file-leader or dew-drier in the early morning prepares the path through the long grasses of the African forest for those that are to follow, so did Isaac Watts go before in the ranks of English hymnists. Up until the close of the 17th century there were no hymns in the church services, only the metrical versions of the Psalms. Dr. Watts changed all that and opened up the way for those that were to follow. It was the dawn of a new day. Isaac

Watts heralded that dawn and has gone down in history as "the father of English hymnody".

Isaac Watts, Southampton's best-remembered son, was born there on July 17th, 1674, the eldest of the family of eight children of Isaac and Sarah Watts. Both his parents were devout Christians, members of the Nonconformist Church, which at that time was enduring great persecution, both from the State and from the Established Church. Isaac Watts (senior) was among those who suffered for their faith and convictions, and at the time of young Isaac's birth was a prisoner in God's House Tower, Southampton.

Isaac, as a boy, was intellectually brilliant with a remarkable passion for learning. From an early age, he started to write verse and in this he was encouraged by his mother; on receiving any monetary award young Isaac would immediately run to his mother with the cry, "A book, a book; buy me a book!". Isaac received early instruction from his father and then studied under Mr. Pinhorne in Southampton where he acquired a good knowledge of Latin, Hebrew, Greek and French. A certain Dr. John Speed of Southampton offered to further Isaac's education at either Oxford or Cambridge University on the condition that he would enter the ministry of the Church of England. Young Isaac, however, declined that offer, threw in his lot with the Dissenters, and entered the Nonconformist Academy at Stoke Newington Green under the charge of Thomas Rowe.

After four years at the Academy, Isaac returned home to Southampton where, for a period of two and a half years, he waited upon God as to directions for his life; he had already been converted at the age of fifteen and had, by this time, consecrated his life to God. During this period at Southampton, it happened that on a certain Sunday after returning from the regular church service, he complained to his father about the poverty of the metrical Psalms as a vehicle of praise to God. "Try then", said his father, "whether you can yourself produce something better". Young Isaac accepted the challenge and wrote "Behold the glories of the Lamb" which was sung by the congregation the following Sunday. Some two hundred of Watts' best hymns were written during this "waiting" period of his life in Southampton.

At the age of twenty-two Watts returned to London, first as tutor to the son of Sir John Hartopp at Newington, then later as assistant to Dr. Chauncey in Mark Lane Church. On Dr.

Chauncey's resignation some years later, Watts took over the pastorate which he held for the remaining forty-six years of his life and during those years Dr. Isaac Watts was renowned by many as London's foremost preacher. His ministry, however, was early interrupted by periods of ill health; the climate of London city he found to be uncongenial.

In 1712, on the invitation of Sir Thomas and Lady Abney, Watts went to Theobalds, their Hertfordshire home for a week's rest and change of surroundings. That week extended into nearly forty years and the remainder of Watts' life was spent as guest and chaplain of that amiable family, first at Theobalds and later at Stoke Newington. The kindness and attention that Watts received from the Abney family brought a great improvement to his health and the seclusion of their mansion homes proved ideal for the continuation of his studies and writing.

Watts' contribution during those years was enormous. Intellectually brilliant and with many advantages he used them all to the glory of God. In the field of education he was a pioneer and was looked up to by all the Dissenting schools and academies of his day; his *Catechism* of instruction for children, his *Divine and Moral Songs, for the Use of Children*, and his *The Improvement of the Mind* were all highly treasured. In the field of astronomy, his *First Principles of Astronomy and Geography* and *The Knowledge of the Heavens and the Earth Made Easy* merited the highest praise. His contribution to literature received recognition from the Universities of Edinburgh and Aberdeen in an honorary doctorate in 1728. His vision and effort laid the basis for the book (later completed by Dr. Philip Doddridge), *The Rise and Progress of Religion in the Soul*, a book judged by many as the most useful of the 18th century. But, first of all, Watts was an evangelist; his greatest concern was to preach the gospel, and though in the pulpit insignificant of stature, he was at the same time a giant in the things of God.

Watts, from the seclusion of the Abney mansions, continued his ministry as health permitted. He kept closely in touch with events in the outside world, and was in many ways a guide to the nation. After his death on November 25th, 1748, at the age of seventy-four, and his burial beside other worthies in Bunhill Fields, a monument was erected to his memory and work in Westminster Abbey.

Few men have left behind such purity of character and such

monuments of laborious piety. Isaac Watts' greatest legacy, however, was his contribution to hymnology. "His poems were his finest works", states David Fountain. "He stands absolutely alone", states Thomas Wright, "He has no peer. He is the greatest of the great". Mr. Wright adds, "If nothing from his pen has attained to the popularity of Toplady's 'Rock of ages' or is quite so affecting as Cowper's 'God moves in a mysterious way'; if he lacks the mellifluence of Charles Wesley or the equipoise of John Newton, the fact remains that he has written a larger number of hymns of the first rank than any other hymnist".

Over six hundred hymns in all have come from Watts' pen, among them some that will never die, as,

> "Alas, and did my Saviour bleed?"
> "Are we the soldiers of the cross?"
> "Behold the glories of the Lamb"
> "Come, let us join our cheerful songs"
> "Come, we that love the Lord"
> "I'm not ashamed to own my Lord"
> "Jesus shall reign, where'er the sun"
> "Join all the glorious names"
> "Not all the blood of beasts"
> "Our God, our help in ages past"
> "There is a land of pure delight"
> "When I survey the wondrous cross".

("Jesus shall reign, where'er the sun" and "Our God, our help in ages past" are in effect Watts' imitations of Psalm 72 and of Psalm 90.)

The sweetest of all Watts' compositions and pronounced by critics as the finest in the English language is his famous and universally loved hymn, "When I survey the wondrous Cross".

> *When I survey the wondrous Cross*
> *On which the Prince of Glory died,*
> *My richest gain I count but loss,*
> *And pour contempt on all my pride.*
>
> *Forbid it, Lord, that I should boast,*
> *Save in the death of Christ, my God;*
> *All the vain things that charm me most,*
> *I sacrifice them to His blood.*

See from His head, His hands, His feet,
Sorrow and love flow mingled down;
Did e'er such love and sorrow meet,
Or thorns compose so rich a crown!

Were the whole realm of nature mine,
That were an off'ring far too small;
Love so amazing, so divine,
Demands my soul, my life, my all.

The singing of these words has touched the hearts of many, many indeed, and without respect or distinction. They reached the empty enquiring heart of Hepsey, the poor gypsy girl, till she enquired as to the meaning of that "love, so amazing, so divine". She listened eagerly to the story of the cross and though she had never heard it before, she drank in its message. Her empty heart was satisfied. That was what she had wanted. Right at the opposite end of society Matthew Arnold, a man of literary fame and with a mind that was cold and critical, was broken and won by these words. He had just listened to Dr. John Watson (better known as Ian Maclaren) preach at Sefton Park in Liverpool on "The Shadow of the Cross". At the close of the service the congregation sang Dr. Watt's heart-reaching hymn. He went to his lodging to ponder its meaning. "Ah, yes", he remarked to Mr. and Mrs. Cropper, "the cross still stands and in the straits of the soul makes its ancient appeal"; within an hour, he had suffered a heart attack and passed away.

In this hymn, Isaac Watts brings us to the cross—the cross of Christ where everything else in life is seen in true perspective. In light of that cross material possessions and the vain charms of life seem as nothing. The sacrifice of the "Prince of Glory" was for the souls of sinful men, and commands from them unreserved surrender of heart and life in return.

His dying crimson, like a robe,
Spreads o'er His body on the tree;
Then am I dead to all the globe,
And all the globe is dead to me.

"Jesus, Thy blood and righteousness"

Count Nicolaus Ludwig von Zinzendorf (1700-1760)

Count Zinzendorf.

The church of Christ owes much to godly mothers and godly grandmothers. It is known that soon after the birth of Nicolaus Ludwig von Zinzendorf on May 26th, 1700, at Dresden, Saxony, Germany, his godly mother in recording the event in her Bible made this prayerful entry, "May the Father of mercies rule the heart of this child, so that he may walk honestly and uprightly. May sin never rule over him, and may his feet be steadfast in the Word; then he will be happy for time and eternity". The boy's father, Count Zinzendorf, who was descended from one of the most ancient, noble and wealthy families in Saxony, and who held office under the Elector of Saxony, died six weeks after the birth of his son. His mother remarried and Nicolaus was brought up by his maternal grandmother, Henriette Catherine von Gersdorf, on her estate at Hennersdorf. She too was a woman of deep piety and talent, a writer of hymns and religious works.

Nicolaus, when he was ten years of age, was sent to the Pietist school of Pastor Francke in Halle and there he spent six years. It would appear that a work of grace in his salvation was effected in those early years for, in looking back to those days from adult life, he recounted "it is more than thirty years since I received a deep impression of Divine grace through the preaching of the cross. The desire to bring souls to Christ took possession of me, and my heart became fixed on the Lamb".

At the age of sixteen, strong pressure was brought to bear upon Nicolaus to embark upon a diplomatic career in State service and he was sent by his guardian-uncle to study law at the University of Wittenberg. He qualified there three years later and was appointed Counsellor of the State at the Court of Saxony. It was just about this time that, in a pressing desire to see the world, he came one evening to the public gallery in Düsseldorf and there, while gazing upon Stenburg's telling picture of the crucifixion was confronted with life's great crisis. The Christ of Calvary seemed to gaze into his very soul and the words of the inscription underneath to burn into his heart.

"All this I did for thee;
What hast thou done for Me?"

Overcome by the love of Christ, he straightway resolved in his heart to serve only Him; thereafter, his life's motto was to be, "I have but one passion and that is **HE** and only **HE**". He had seen the Christ, but more, he had also seen the world, not in its luxury but in its need and he resolved to do something about it.

In the early 18th century many Moravian and Bohemian believers, suffering under an oppressive Austrian government, fled their country and sought freedom under Zinzendorf on his estate at Berthelsdorf. These followers of John Huss (the "old goose of Bohemia") were welcomed and one of their leaders,

Christian David, founded there the famous colony of Herrnhut (meaning "the protection of the Lord"). This model village was soon renowned far and wide, and Zinzendorf was famed for his willingness to receive all oppressed believers. Zinzendorf loved them as brethren in Christ and ministered fervently and untiringly in their midst. His biographer tells of his last days at Herrnhut, how that he endeavoured to seek the personal acquaintance of every member therein, whereby he might ascertain their spiritual state before God and that there was scarcely one soul there that he did not converse with privately.

Zinzendorf's dedication and vision inspired the Moravians to become pioneers in foreign missions. In the year 1732, when the Herrnhut colony numbered about six hundred, two of its number were sent forth as missionaries to the island of St. Thomas in the West Indies. When they departed, each with six dollars in his pocket, they determined to sell themselves as slaves if that was the only way of bringing the gospel to the negroes. In this spirit, the Moravian missions grew and grew, reaching to all five continents of the world. Thus, years before William Carey sailed for India or John Wesley itinerated around his native England, the Moravians had one hundred and sixty-five missions scattered throughout the world.

Zinzendorf also became a prolific hymn-writer and is reckoned to have been one of the greatest in Germany. His first hymn was written as a boy at Halle in 1712, his last just a few days before he died at Herrnhut in 1760, and between these dates he wrote more than two thousand hymns in all. His critics maintain that he wrote too much and did not give enough care to revision and correction. Nevertheless, some of his hymns are of excellent worth, fired by a deep personal devotion to his Saviour and marked by simplicity and sweetness.

Zinzendorf died at Herrnhut on May 9th, 1760. His closing testimony was assuring and triumphant, "I am going to the Saviour, I am ready. If He is no longer willing to make use of me here, I am ready to go to Him, for I have nothing else to keep me here". Thus he passed away into the presence of his Lord. It is recorded that there were scarcely sufficient funds to pay for his grave and yet many travelled from long distances to pay last respects to a great leader. Over two thousand attended his funeral and several of his own hymns were sung on that occasion.

The hymns of Count Zinzendorf were sung at the first by the Moravians at Herrnhut colony and later by Moravians worldwide. It was the singing of these hymns that captured the hearts and influenced so deeply the lives of John and Charles Wesley. When they first heard them on a visit to Herrnhut and later on board ship to Georgia in America, their hearts were stirred, not only by the spiritual richness and depth of the words, but by the fervour and abandon with which they were sung.

Zinzendorf's hymns today are to be found mostly in Moravian collections but two of his compositions have found much wider acceptance and acclaim. "Jesus, still lead me on", known in its original by almost every Sunday-school child in Germany has been translated into the English by Miss Jane Borthwick. "Jesus, Thy blood and righteousness", written by Zinzendorf in 1739 while returning from a visit to his missionary friends in the West Indies and rendered the following year into English by John Wesley, is the hymn by which he is best remembered. In its original there were thirty-three verses and some of these will ever have an enduring place in the hearts of the people of God.

> Jesus, Thy blood and righteousness,
> My beauty are, my glorious dress;
> Midst flaming worlds, in these arrayed,
> With joy shall I lift up my head.
>
> This spotless robe the same appears,
> When ruined nature sinks in years;
> No age can change its glorious hue,
> The robe of Christ is ever new.
>
> When from the dust of death I rise
> To claim my mansion in the skies,
> E'en then shall this be all my plea—
> Jesus hath lived, hath died for me!
>
> Lord, I believe, were sinners more
> Than sands upon the ocean shore,
> Thou hast for all a ransom paid,
> For all a full atonement made.

Ah! give to all Thy servants, Lord,
With power to speak Thy gracious word,
That all who to Thy wounds will flee,
May find eternal life in Thee.

Man, through the Fall, divested of his white and honourable robe of perfect innocence appears cringing before his God in his spiritual nakedness. Our Bible, however, declares that his God is none other than Jehovah Tsidkenu (Jer. 23:6) and that He hath provided for His creature "a robe of righteousness" (Isa. 61:10). Like the inner vestment of the Saviour this robe of righteousness is without seam, woven throughout. Many eyes, human, angelic, satanic and even Divine have scrutinized it; it is without flaw and without spot. Such is the sufficiency of Calvary's work that the believer's spiritual attire is complete and he now appears unashamed and resplendent before his God: nor will this robe of righteousness ever fade or wear out with the passing of time or throughout a long eternity!

My beauty this, my glorious dress
Jesus, Thy blood and righteousness!

"O happy day that fixed my choice"

Philip Doddridge (1702-1751)

Philip Doddridge.

Philip Doddridge was the twentieth child of his parents and was so feeble at birth that no one expected him to live. However, he survived and grew up to become one of the most godly and revered men of the 18th century. Both his parents were devout believers in the Lord Jesus. His father was an oilman by trade. His mother was the daughter of a Lutheran clergyman who, under bitter persecution, had fled from Bohemia to England. Young Philip was brought up in the nurture of the Lord, his mother teaching him the

47

Holy Scriptures before he could read. Bible characters and scenes were portrayed on the blue Dutch hearth tiles of their "Puritan" home and many of Philip's early lessons were taken from them.

Philip's father and mother died when he was young and at thirteen he entered a private school at St. Albans. There the local minister, Dr. Samuel Clark, a Noncomformist, took a deep interest in the lad and acted as a second father to him. When only a boy, Philip felt called of God to enter the Christian ministry but as an orphan lad without means he saw no possibility of his hope ever being fulfilled. At sixteen years of age, the Duchess of Bedford made an approach to him offering to pay for all his education provided he would enter the ministry of the Church of England, but Philip declined that generous offer of the Duchess and threw in his lot with the Dissenters. He sought the Lord's guidance and help through fervent prayer and one day while on his bended knees, a communication reached him from a Dr. Clark offering to assist him in his training. In later life, Doddridge often praised God for this "so seasonable an interposition of Divine Providence". He entered Jennings' Nonconformist Academy at Kibworth, Leicestershire, and finished his studies at Hinckley. When at Hinckley, Doddridge preached his first sermon as a young man of twenty years of age, taking as his text 1 Cor. 16:22, "If any man love not the Lord Jesus, let him be Anathema Maran-atha". God blessed that first message and as the result two souls were converted to God. Very shortly afterwards, he accepted his first charge at Kibworth and there he remained for the next seven years.

In 1729, Doddridge received a call to Castle Hill Meeting in Northampton but for a time was reluctant to move away from his flock at Kibworth to the larger responsibility in Northampton. However, God through some very striking circumstances soon made the pathway clear to him and thus convinced that he should follow the Divine leading, he moved to Northampton and there he spent the remaning years of his life. His ministry at Northampton was his real life's work and through his efforts an academy was opened, where over the subsequent years, some two hundred students prepared themselves for the Dissenting ministry. At the academy due attention was always given to sermon preparation— "May I remember that I am not here to acquire a reputation but to dispense the gospel which my Redeemer brought from Heaven and sealed with His blood".

Doddridge was ever wise and kind; he was filled with unaffected goodness and had wide sympathies. In that city he made many friends and through these friendships won many of them for Christ. James Stonhouse, a young doctor of academic brilliance and limitless energies, had just then come to Northampton. This very attentive and popular young doctor was an avowed atheist. Doddridge courted his friendship and that strangely-assorted pair were thereafter often linked together in enterprising work in Northampton. They were the means of establishing a hospital in the town, something almost unknown in those days outside of the city of London. One day, a lady in her final illness summoned both Dr. Doddridge and Dr. Stonhouse to her bedside and requested that Doddridge should preach her funeral sermon and that Stonhouse would attend. Though Stonhouse had never before been in a place of worship, he consented to go. He kept his promise and through that message God spoke to his unbelieving heart. As a result he renounced his infidelity and was converted to Christ. Writing to a friend afterwards of that great event, Stonhouse stated in his letter, "the blessed instrument employed by God for effecting this great work was Dr. Doddridge".

Another incident in the historic ministry of Dr. Doddridge in Northampton is full of interest. An Irishman named O'Connell was convicted of a capital offence and condemned to die. Dr. Doddridge at great trouble and expense thoroughly investigated his case and was convinced of O'Connell's innocence. Judgment, however, had been given and a reprieve could not be granted. On the day of his execution, O'Connell made a final request—that the cart carrying him to the gallows might stop for a few moments at Dr. Doddridge's door. His request was granted. In that solemn moment, he knelt on the minister's doorstep and in the presence of a great crowd was heard to say, "Dr. Doddridge, every hair of my head thanks you; every throb of my heart thanks you; every drop of my blood thanks you; for you did your best to save me!"

Dr. Philip Doddridge held a very close friendship throughout life with Dr. Isaac Watts, though Watts was by thirty years his senior, and stemming from that friendship came an outstanding literary work, *The Rise and Progress of Religion in the Soul*, judged by many as the most useful book of the 18th century. It was translated into many languages and the reading of it reached and transformed the sinful heart of the young William Wilberforce who later became the emancipator of the slaves. Doddridge's other famous literary work, *The Family Expositor*, was the product of many years of devotion and toil and is a commentary on the entire New Testament. In recognition of Doddridge's literary ability and contributions, the University of Aberdeen conferred on him an honorary doctorate.

Doddridge, as a minister of the gospel, was greatly used of God. He was a text preacher and to impress his text upon the hearts of his hearers, he composed an appropriate hymn to accompany his message. The first stanza of the hymn was given to introduce the subject, then the sermon was preached and at the close the complete hymn was sung by the congregation. In this way most of Dr. Doddridge's hymns came to be written. They were not published in his lifetime but circulated widely in manuscript form. After Doddridge's death in 1751, Job Orton, his lifelong friend and biographer collected his hymns and published them in 1755 as *Hymns Founded on Various Texts in the Holy Scriptures, by the late Philip Doddridge, D.D.* That 1755 collection contained three hundred and seventy-five hymns. In 1839 a great-grandson, John Doddridge, re-edited the hymns from the original manuscripts and this work contained twenty-two additional hymns. Dr. James Hamilton wrote of Doddridge's hymns, "at once beautiful and buoyant, these sacred strains are destined to convey the devout emotions of Doddridge to every shore where his Master is loved and where his mother-tongue is spoken".

Doddridge's hymns in common usage today appear in various church hymnals and at least three are familiar to believers in assembly gatherings—"O happy day that fixed my choice", "Grace 'tis a charming sound", and "O God of Bethel, by whose hand". This last mentioned was David Livingstone's favourite hymn and he was often cheered by it during his lonely wanderings in central Africa; when at last his remains were brought to Westminster Abbey, it was the hymn chosen to be sung beside his grave.

· The hymn, "O happy day that fixed my choice", is a great favourite of many. In its original it consisted of five stanzas without a refrain.

> *O happy day that fixed my choice*
> *On Thee, my Saviour and my God:*

Well may this glowing heart rejoice,
And tell its raptures all abroad.

O happy bond, that seals my vows
To Him who merits all my love:
Let cheerful anthems fill His house,
While to that sacred shrine I move.

'Tis done, the great transaction's done;
I am my Lord's, and He is mine:
He drew me, and I followed on,
Charmed to confess the voice divine.

Now rest, my long-divided heart,
Fixed on this blissful centre, rest:
With ashes who would grudge to part,
When called on angels' bread to feast?

High heaven, that heard the solemn vow,
That vow renewed shall daily hear:
Till in life's latest hour I bow,
And bless in death a bond so dear.

Dr. Doddridge entitled his hymn, "Rejoicing in our Covenant Engagements with God". The words epitomise the whole life-experience of the author. As a boy in his early teens he had made a covenant with God; from year to year he had reviewed it, asking God's pardon for failure to keep it as faithfully as he desired, and "in life's latest hour", in the final stages of consumption at Lisbon on October 26th, 1751, when his wife noticed his lips moving and asked if he wanted anything he replied, "No, I am only renewing my covenant engagements with God".

"Blessed is the man", says James Montgomery, "that can take the words of this hymn and make them his own from personal experience".

"And can it be that I should gain"

Charles Wesley (1707-1788)

Charles Wesley.

The face of 18th century England was changed by two brothers—John and Charles Wesley. They were the two youngest surviving sons of the very large family of Samuel and Susanna Wesley. Both were born at Epworth Rectory in Lincolnshire; both were greatly used of the Lord in their respective and complementary roles during the nation-wide spiritual revival of their day, and both are now enshrined side by side among England's great in Westminster Abbey.

At the beginning of the 18th century, church life in England was neglected and corrupt; the clergy were worldlings, church services were frequently omitted and parish visitation almost unknown. At Epworth, however, things were different for there Samuel Wesley sought to fulfil a faithful ministry for God. Though poor in circumstances and often lacking the bare necessities of life, his faith and morals were of the highest standard and he sought to impart the same, both to his parishioners and to his own family. But, perhaps, the central figure of that home at Epworth rectory was the mother, Susanna Wesley, a woman remarkable in faith and diligence, who cared meticulously for the physical and spiritual welfare of each one of her children. Susanna Wesley made herself personally responsible for the education of her sons until they went away to school and, thereafter, she pursued them with earnest letters. In writing to her youngest son, Charles, she spoke to him exultantly of her Saviour, "Oh, my dear Charles, when I consider the dignity of His person, the perfection of His purity, the greatness of His sufferings but, above all, His boundless love, I am astonished and utterly confounded. I am lost in thought. I fall into nothing before Him". And having such a mother as Susanna Wesley, the Wesley children were blessed indeed!

Charles Wesley, at the age of eight, left home for Westminster School in London. He became captain of the school and after ten years gained a "studentship" to Christ Church, Oxford. He was a brilliant classical scholar and took his M.A. degree at the age of twenty-two. The following six years were spent at Oxford as a college tutor and then, in company with his brother John, he left England for Georgia in North America. His experience there was very disappointing and he soon returned to England.

Charles Wesley's spiritual awakening and conversion to God took place soon after his return to England. As he lay ill in the home of a friend in London, he was visited by the influential Moravian, Peter Böhler. "Do you hope to be saved?" Böhler enquired. "I do", replied Charles and Böhler asked upon what ground. "On the ground that I have used my best endeavours to serve God", Charles answered, whereupon Böhler shook his head, obviously dissatisfied. This simple encounter was used by the Lord to impress upon the heart of Charles Wesley his need of personal salvation. He sought it and found it. That never-to-be-forgotten experience took place on Sunday, May 21st, 1738. As

Mrs. Turner, a poor Moravian woman, spoke to him words of light and life, he exclaimed, "I believe, I believe".

On that very same day, Charles read from his *Book of Common Prayer* the words of Psalm 40, "He hath put a new song in my mouth, even a thanksgiving unto our God". These words were prophetic, for in the fifty years that followed, Charles Wesley wrote no less than six thousand five hundred new songs of praise to God (the equivalent of one new song every three days for fifty years). From 1738-1788, in conjunction with his brother John, he issued thirty-nine different books of hymns and poetry.

Charles Wesley's hymns are not only numerous but many are of a very high quality. Dr. J. H. Overton's considered opinion is that, "taking quantity and quality into consideration, Charles Wesley, perhaps, is the great hymn-writer of all ages". Dr. J. W. Bready's testimony is that, Charles Wesley's ministry "gave to the English-speaking world its richest heritage of sacred song". A natural aptitude to express things in verse, a complete classical education and a sense of spiritual urgency resulted in compositions, many of which will never die. Will the Church of God ever exhaust this spiritual richness or will it ever grow weary of singing such majestic hymns as Wesley's, "Jesus, lover of my soul", "Oh, for a thousand tongues to sing!", "Hark! the herald angels sing" or "Love divine, all loves excelling"? Mr. Bernard Manning records that, "Wesley is obsessed with the greatest things, and he confirms our faith because he shows us these things above all the immediate, local, fashionable problems and objections to our faith. We move into the serener air. We sit in the heavenly places with Christ Jesus", and he adds, "Wesley's hymns . . . show us something of the life of one of the pure in heart who saw God".

Charles Wesley wrote when religious revival swept the country. As his brother John rode up and down the English countryside on horseback preaching the everlasting gospel, Charles set that epoch-making revival to deathless music. Dr. F. W. Boreham says, "John set the country weeping, Charles set it singing, and those tears of bitter repentance and those songs of plenteous redemption were the outward and visible evidence of the mightiest spiritual surge in the nation's experience", and he adds, "the movement that brought new life to the world in the 18th century stands crystallised in the throbbing verse of Charles Wesley".

From the moment of conversion to God, hymns started to flow

from Charles Wesley's pen and these continued right until his death on March 29th, 1788. At the age of eighty when he could no longer write, and just a short time before he died, he dictated to his wife his final hymn and entitled it "A Last Wish". It is only a single stanza but full of pathos and beauty.

> *In age and feebleness extreme,*
> *Who shall a helpless worm redeem?*
> *Jesus! my only hope Thou art,*
> *Strength of my failing flesh and heart*
> *O could I catch one smile from Thee*
> *And drop into eternity!*

Christ, the Redeemer of men, was ever his theme. "Jesus! my only hope" he cries as he comes to the close. It was likewise so at the beginning; the thought of "the Saviour and His blood" had thrilled his soul when he first lifted his pen and wrote for us words that will never die.

> *And can it be that I should gain,*
> *   An interest in the Saviour's blood?*
> *Died He for me who caused His pain?*
> *   For me who Him to death pursued?*
> *Amazing love! how can it be*
> *That Thou, my God, shouldst die for me!*
>
> *'Tis mystery all! the Immortal dies;*
> *   Who can explore His strange design?*
> *In vain the first-born seraph tries*
> *   To sound the depths of love divine;*
> *'Tis mercy all! let earth adore,*
> *Let angel minds inquire no more.*
>
> *He left His Father's throne above—*
> *   So free, so infinite His grace—*
> *Emptied Himself of all but love,*
> *   And bled for Adam's helpless race.*
> *'Tis mercy all, immense and free;*
> *For, O my God, it found out me!*

Long my imprisoned spirit lay
  Fast bound in sin and nature's night;
Thine eye diffused a quickening ray—
  I woke, the dungeon flamed with light;
My chains fell off, my heart was free,
I rose, went forth, and followed Thee.

No condemnation now I dread;
  Jesus, and all in Him, is mine!
Alive in Him, my living Head,
  And clothed in righteousness divine,
Bold I approach the eternal throne,
And claim the crown, through Christ, my own.

The theme of Charles Wesley's hymn is the grace of God. In sovereign majesty and at infinite cost, Divine grace has sped its way downward from the throne to the darkness of the dungeon, and with its coveted and gotten prize soared again back to the heights of the throne. That someone so worthless as he should have been the prize of such infinite grace was for Charles Wesley a staggering thought. Nevertheless he knew it to be true and poured forth his heart's ecstasy in the words of this immortal hymn.

"How good is the God we adore"

Joseph Hart (1712-1768)

HYMNS, &c.

COMPOSED ON

Various Subjects.

By J. HART.

O *sing unto the Lord a new Song; for he hath done* MARVELLOUS THINGS: *His right Hand, and his holy Arm hath gotten him the Victory.* Pfalm xcviii. 1.

THE SEVENTH EDITION, With the AUTHOR'S EXPERIENCE, the SUPPLEMENT, and APPENDIX.

LONDON:

Printed by M. LEWIS, in Pater-nofter-Row; And fold by F. NEWBERY, at the Crown, the corner of St. Paul's Church-Yard, Ludgate-Hill; and by the AUTHOR'S WIDOW, (the Lamb) near Durham-Yard, in the Strand; and at the MEETINGS in Jewin-Street, and Bartholomew-Clofe.

Price bound Two-Shillings.

Title page of Joseph Hart's hymns, 1770 (7th Ed.).

How good is the God we adore,
    Our faithful unchangeable Friend!
His love is as great as His power,
    And knows neither measure nor end!

'Tis Jesus, the First and the Last,
    Whose Spirit shall guide us safe home;
We'll praise Him for all that is past,
    And trust Him for all that's to come.

These lines were written by Joseph Hart. They are, in fact, but a single stanza taken from a lengthy poem, "No prophet, nor dreamer of dreams", based on the opening verses of Deut. 13. The form of the first line, as originally written by Hart was, "This God is the God we adore"; in some collections it is found as, "This, this is the God we adore".

Joseph Hart lived in the 18th century. He was "born of believing parents" in the city of London in 1712. Educationally he received a good start in life and later became a teacher of "the learned languages". Spiritually, however, things were very different, Julian describing his early life as, "a curious mixture of loose conduct, serious conviction of sin and endeavourings after amendment of life". For many years his experience appears to have alternated between periods of conviction of sin and periods of gross indulgences. But let Hart tell of his spiritual experience in his own words.

"On entering manhood, I advanced to dreadful heights of libertinism, and ran to such dangerous lengths of carnal and spiritual wickedness that I even outwent professed infidels and shocked the irreligious and profane with my blasphemies... In this abominable state I continued a bold-faced rebel for nine years, not only committing acts of lewdness myself, but infecting others with all the poison of my delusions... After a time I fell into a deep despondency of mind, and, shunning all company, I went about bewailing my sad and dark condition.

"In this sad state I went moping about till Whit Sunday, 1757, when I happened to go in the afternoon to the Moravian Chapel in Fetter Lane. The minister preached from Rev. 3:10. I was much impressed."

"I was hardly got home, when I felt myself melting away into a strange softness of affection which made me fling myself on my knees before God. My horrors were immediately expelled, and such comfort flowed into my heart as no words can paint... I cried out, 'What, me, Lord?' His Spirit answered in me, 'Yes, thee!' I objected, 'But I have been so unspeakably evil and wicked!' The answer was, 'I pardon thee freely and fully!' The alteration I then felt in my soul was as sudden and palpable as that which is experienced by a person staggering and almost sinking under a burden, when it is immediately taken from his shoulders. Tears ran in streams from my eyes for a considerable while, and I was so swallowed up in joy and thankfulness that I hardly knew where I was. I threw myself willingly into my Saviour's hands, lay weeping at His feet...". Hart at that time was forty-five years of age.

Conversion's experience brought tremendous changes. Though there were many temptations, Hart walked humbly with God and applied himself in earnest to the preaching of the gospel and to the writing of hymns and poems. These were published in 1759 as *Hymns Composed on Various Subjects*; in the preface of this volume there is a brief account of the author's spiritual experience.

In 1760, Hart became minister of an Independent Chapel in London, the "Old Wooden Meeting-House in Jewin Street", built nearly a century before by William Jenkyn. There he ministered regularly, faithfully and fruitfully to a large congregation who looked on him as an "earnest, eloquent and much-loved" minister of the gospel.

Hart's ministry in Jewin Street continued for eight years, right up to the close of his life. He died on May 24th, 1768, at the early age of fifty-six and was buried in Bunhill Fields. There, a large crowd of some twenty thousand people gathered to pay their last respects to a much-loved minister of the gospel, and at his funeral service it was said, "He was like the laborious ox that dies with the yoke on his neck; so died he with the yoke of Christ on his neck; neither would he suffer it to be taken off; for ye are his witnesses that he preached Christ to you, with the arrows of death sticking in him". So revered was the memory of Joseph Hart that more than a century later (in 1875) an obelisk was erected over his grave in Bunhill Fields.

In the few years from conversion to the close of life Joseph Hart wrote a considerable number of hymns but, apart from a very few, most of these have now disappeared from common usage. His hymns have a spiritual quality of their own and most are based on his own experience, "all the emotions of a soul 'ready to halt', but knowing where to look for strength, are plentifully and feelingly represented".

Hart's hymn, "Come, ye sinners, poor and wretched" is well known to many; it is much used in gospel work and its lines have often brought timely help to troubled souls.

> Let not conscience make you linger,
> Nor of fitness fondly dream;

All the fitness He requireth
Is to feel your need of Him:
This He gives you;
'Tis the Spirit's rising beam.

His hymn on Gethsemane, "Come, all ye chosen saints of God", was born out of an unforgettable personal spiritual experience—a contemplation of the agony of the Saviour in the Garden. It was written in two parts and contained twenty-four stanzas. Two of its lines, full of mystery, majesty and meaning still live on,

Gethsemane, the Olive-Press!
And why so call'd, let angels* guess.

Hart's poem on the Word of God is worthy of mention, though not so widely known. Its lines are pithy and penetrating.

Revere the sacred page,
*   To injure any part*
Betrays, with blind and feeble rage,
*   A hard and haughty heart.*

The Scriptures and the Lord
*   Bear one tremendous Name:*
The Written, and th' Incarnate Word
*   In all things are the same.*

"How Good is the God we adore" is, however, the best known of all Hart's compositions and through the years has often been sung at gatherings of the Lord's people as a fitting expression of deep gratitude to God.

Its words depict the pilgrim on the pathway of pilgrimage. He halts and reflects, "God has been good and faithful; love has ever been the expression of His heart, constancy the hallmark of His friendship. In addition the Lord Jesus in the plenitude of His person and the gracious guiding Spirit of God have been unfailing escorts through all the way". He feels that he has been truly blessed. He raises his "Ebenezer", then steps out into the unknown future, assured that what his Divine Companions have been in the past, so They will be to the end of the road—enough for all the journey.

*"*Christians*" in original.

"Guide me, O Thou great Jehovah"

William Williams (1717-1791)

William Williams.

Wales has always been a land of song. Perhaps no other country in the world has a finer singing tradition and few have superior riches in tunes. When spiritual revival swept that land in the 18th century, it seemed as if a long winter had ended; spring-time had arrived. Throughout the land at that time, a new spirit of song was awakened as never before, and the voice towering above all the others was that of William Williams of Pantycelyn. He was the outstanding hymn-writer of the great revival. Dr. Elvet Lewis in his *Sweet Singers of Wales* states, "What Paul Gerhardt has been to Germany, what Isaac Watts has been to England, that and more William Williams has been to the little Principality of Wales. His hymns have both stirred and soothed the whole nation for more than one hundred years; they have helped to fashion a nation's character and to deepen a nation's piety". William Williams has gone down in history as "The Sweet Singer of Wales".

William Williams, the fourth child of John and Dorothy Williams, was born in 1717 at Cefn-y-coed near Llandovery, Carmarthenshire. When William was a young man, the family moved to an adjacent and more prosperous farm at Pantycelyn and this homestead remains to the present day the family home of the same Williams' family. Thus Pantycelyn and William Williams became inextricably identified with each other; he exists for us today as "Williams Pantycelyn".

William Williams as a boy received a good education. His parents planned that he should become a doctor and as a medical student he was sent to Llwyn-llwyd Academy about thirty miles from home. It happened that one day as he was returning from college on horseback, and passing through Talgarth, Breconshire, he was arrested by the oratory of an open-air preacher mounted on a tombstone within the churchyard wall. He had never heard anything like it before but, as he records later, it was a voice evidently "from Heaven" to his soul. Howel Harris, the young Methodist evangelist, was the preacher that day and his message brought salvation to Williams, then a medical student of twenty years of age.

Within a few days of conversion's experience, Williams became convinced that God would have him give up medical studies and become a physician of souls. He was appointed a deacon of the Church of England at the age of twenty-three and for three years served two small curacies in South Wales. Williams, however, incurred the displeasure of the ruling bishop by his evangelical views, by his going outside his own parish to preach the gospel and by his association with such Dissenters and Revivalists as George Whitefield. Those offences the bishop could not tolerate and Williams was refused full ordination as a priest.

Williams all the while had been ill at ease within the Established Church and was happy to throw in his lot with fellow Revivalists, taking all Wales as his parish. In association with Howel Harris of

Trefeca, Daniel Rowland of Llangeitho and Howel Davies of Pembrokeshire, he moved up and down the country like a flame, arousing the people to a consciousness of their sin and need of a Saviour, and mightily was he used of God, though suffering persecution in many parts. Howel Harris wrote of him, "Hell trembles when Williams comes, and souls are taken daily by Brother Williams in the gospel-net". In about half a century he travelled some one hundred thousand miles throughout the Principality on horse-back or on foot proclaiming the glorious gospel. He died in his home at Pantycelyn on January 11th, 1791, at the age of seventy-four, after a long and painful illness—honoured, much respected and indeed greatly loved. He was laid to rest in Llanfair-ar-y-bryn Churchyard, Llandovery; a visitor to that spot today may there see his tombstone and read from the epitaph:

"William Williams"
"A sinner saved"

"He awaits here the coming of the Morning Star"

William Williams may be described as a truly great man. Besides being a great theologian, he was a great preacher; besides being a great poet (reckoned by some authorities as the greatest of all Welsh poets), he was a great hymn-writer. In his hymns, numbering about eight hundred and sixty in all, we have the combination of truly great poetry and perfect theology. He wrote almost entirely in Welsh; his works are not easily or successfully translated, so his greatness as a hymn-writer cannot be truly assessed or appreciated, except by the Welsh people themselves.

Springing as he did from a rural background, Williams drew widely for his compositions from nature around him—the dawn, the sunset, the mountains, the harvest field, a summer's evening, a winter's night, a clear morning after a storm or a quiet haven by the sea; these he used to reflect the experience of the soul, believing that the book of nature harmonised fully with the revelation of Scripture.

Williams' hymns were a mighty influence among the Welsh people of the 18th century, for many who could not themselves read soon learned his hymns and thousands of people knew a great many of them by heart. Such was their spiritual content that the common people used them more for private meditation than for community singing.

Of the very few of Williams' hymns which we have in English today, the greatest and most widely known is, "Guide me, O Thou great Jehovah". Originally written in Welsh, it consisted of five verses and was first published in 1745. Some years later, Peter Williams (no relation) translated three verses into English. This translation, however, did not entirely satisfy William Williams, its original composer. He, himself, therefore rewrote the hymn in English, preserving the first verse much as Peter Williams had rendered it but rewriting completely the second and third verses.

> Guide me, O Thou great Jehovah,
>   Pilgrim through this barren land;
> I am weak, but Thou art mighty,
>   Hold me with Thy powerful hand:
>   Bread of heaven!
>   Feed me till I want no more.
>
> Open now the crystal fountain,
>   Whence the healing stream doth flow;
> Let the fire and cloudy pillar
>   Lead me all my journey through:
>   Strong deliverer!
>   Be Thou still my strength and shield.
>
> When I tread the verge of Jordan,
>   Bid my anxious fears subside;
> Death of deaths, and hell's destruction,
>   Land me safe on Canaan's side:
>   Songs of praises
>   I will ever give to Thee.

The lovely Welsh tune, "Cwm Rhondda", to which this hymn is sung today was composed by John Hughes in 1907. The hymn and the tune are complementary, indeed, almost inseparably linked, and have a universal appeal. Welsh men are unrivalled singers of this hymn and especially in the open air. Besides, the hymn has now been translated into seventy-five other languages.

The imagery of the hymn is based on the forty years' journey of the Israelites through the wilderness to the land of Canaan. Williams, in his hymn, identifies himself with the pilgrims to Canaan and, appreciating the tortuosity and dangers of the way, he solicits the guidance, the care and the protection of the God of Israel. As through the wilderness the pilgrim makes his way, his eye and heart are lifted to Heaven, "Guide me ... Hold me ... Feed me ..."; so he proceeds to the better land. Truly Williams' hymn is the prayer of the pilgrim!

"In evil long I took delight"

John Newton (1725-1807)

John Newton.

John Newton almost lost his life in a violent storm in the mid Atlantic. John Newton almost lost his soul on the tempestuous sea of life. When tossed upon life's billows and finding the strong under-currents and the hidden rocks too treacherous for him, he was miraculously saved by an Almighty Hand, and ever afterward delighted to tell of the amazing delivering grace of God.

John Newton commenced the voyage of life at Wapping on the Thames on July 24th, 1725. He was the only child of a strict and stern sea-captain and of a caring, godly mother. Elizabeth Newton protected her boy from every appearance of evil, prayed faithfully for him and took him regularly to a little Dissenting Chapel in Radcliffe Square where Dr. Isaac Watts' hymns were sung in the church services. Watts' great hymn, "When I survey the wondrous Cross" left a deep impression on the young boy's mind. It was Elizabeth Newton's supreme wish that her son would one day become a minister of the gospel, though his father, on the other hand, desired for John a career at sea.

Ere John had reached his seventh birthday, his mother died and his father promptly married again. Captain Newton's sea-faring life took him away much from home and, as a consequence, John was left virtually an orphan. At home, he was unloved; at school he suffered the cane and birch rod under a tyrant headmaster; boyhood days held few joys for John Newton.

When only eleven years of age, John was taken to sea by his father and there the spiritual impressions of early childhood soon became eroded. By the age of seventeen, poisonous seeds of infidelity were sown in his mind; those seeds, from Shaftesbury's book, Characteristics, found fertile soil and took root, and John set out on a path to follow the dictates of his own heart and mind. Six terrible profligate years followed. At eighteen, he was seized by the Naval Press and put on board H.M.S. Harwich. There, midst naval profaneness and debauchery, he encountered a "friend", a free thinker, named Mitchell, who poured the poison of atheism into his fertile mind. Newton became an ardent disciple and thenceforth set out to poison other young minds with this devilish doctrine.

He deserted from the Royal Navy and was arrested, publicly stripped, flogged and degraded. Feeling embittered by such humiliation, he then planned to murder his sea-captain and afterward commit suicide; in all this God over-ruled and his plans were averted. He was then boarded another ship, engaged in the slave trade, and set sail for West Africa to become involved in "that vile traffic of the slave trade" (as he afterwards called it) where slaves, male and female, were collected and bought on the West African coast. These slaves were then boarded ship, branded and fettered at the ship's furnace and transported across the Atlantic; there they were sold on the West Indian sugar estates, where they were destined to endure the tortures of the cart-whip for the few remaining years of their lives. Newton treated those slaves brutally; the fetters, the iron collars, the thumbscrews—he used them all. Among the female slaves, he allowed his lust to run unchecked. Looking back on those years afterwards, he summed them up in the words of 2 Peter 2:14, "Having eyes full of adultery, and that cannot cease from sin; beguiling unstable souls".

Newton, however, sunk to deeper depths. In West Africa he came under the domination of an African woman who disdained him and he was compelled to beg his daily morsel of bread. He was then fettered and chained in solitary confinement till he hoped he would die. John Newton was brought low, truly "a servant of slaves in Africa". Later he described his state as, "depressed to a degree beyond common wretchedness". "I chose the ways of transgressors which I found very hard; they led to slavery, contempt, famine and despair".

Newton's unforgettable spiritual awakening came as he crossed the Atlantic on board the *Greyhound* bound for England. On the voyage he had been reading Thomas à Kempis on the sweetness of the fellowship of Christ and of the judgment of the Great Day for mankind when a thought flashed into his mind, "What if these things should be true!". He pushed the thought from him, closed the book, chatted to his mates and fell asleep. But he was soon awakened by a most violent storm. The *Greyhound* had become a wreck; she was quickly filling with water and about to sink. Newton got to the pumps. He now feared death. His past came up before him; it was black. He found himself speaking to the captain of the mercy of the Lord, but for a wretch like him, what mercy could there be? He began to pray. His thoughts at that moment may be paraphrased from his later writings, "I needed an Almighty Saviour to step in. I found such a One. Jesus, on the Cross, met my need exactly". That hour "he first believed". It was March 10th, 1748, and Newton was then twenty-two years of age.

Many "dangers, toils and snares", however, still lay ahead on the pathway for John Newton, but the abundant grace of God that saved him proved for him sufficient grace for the remainder of the journey of life. He came under the influence of godly Captain Alex Clunie in St. Kitts, and, later of Whitefield and Wesley in England, and through remarkable circumstances was ordained to preach the glorious gospel which he had once laboured to destroy and to extol the precious Name of Jesus which he had once so vehemently blasphemed.

John Newton never allowed himself nor the world to forget the super-abounding and sovereign grace of God that stopped and rescued him on his wild career. Throughout life, as a constant reminder, he kept a text of scripture hanging above the mantelpiece in his study, "Thou shalt remember that thou wast a bondman in the land of Egypt, and the Lord thy God redeemed thee" (Deut. 15:15). When he was an old man, he complained to William Jay of Bath that his faculties were failing him. "My memory", he said, "is nearly gone; but I remember two things—that I am a great sinner, and that Christ is a great Saviour". In the same spirit he penned his own epitaph, which later was inscribed on a tablet in the Church of St. Mary Woolnoth, in the City of London,

JOHN NEWTON
Clerk,
Once an Infidel and Libertine,
a servant of Slaves in Africa,
was
by the rich Mercy of our Lord and Saviour
Jesus Christ
Preserved, Restored, Pardoned,
and Appointed to Preach the Faith
he had long laboured to destroy.

Newton's terrible past sheds much light and lends new meaning to many of the hymns which he wrote; the thought of the profligate years of youth served to magnify the super-abounding and sovereign grace of God; memories of past blasphemies made the precious Name of Jesus increasingly sweet. Few had degraded that Name more than he, and few would excel more than he in exaltation of that same precious Name.

> *How sweet the Name of Jesus sounds*
> *In a believer's ear!*
> *It soothes his sorrows, heals his wounds,*
> *And drives away his fear.*

> It makes the wounded spirit whole,
>   And calms the troubled breast;
> 'Tis manna to the hungry soul,
>   And to the weary rest.

Newton's hymns of personal testimony are hymns that extol the grace of God. Of these, "Amazing Grace" is the best known and is the hymn with which he is most often associated.

> Amazing Grace! How sweet the sound
>   That saved a wretch like me;
> I once was lost, but now am found,
>   Was blind, but now I see.

> 'Twas grace that taught my heart to fear,
>   And grace my fears relieved;
> How precious did that grace appear
>   The hour I first believed!

"In evil long I took delight" is another testimony hymn, equally forceful and magnificent, but perhaps less well known.

> In evil long I took delight
>   Unawed by shame or fear,
> Till a new object met my sight,
>   And stopped my wild career.

> I saw One hanging on a tree
>   In agonies and blood,
> Who fixed His languid eyes on me
>   As near His cross I stood.

> Sure never till my latest breath
>   Can I forget that look;
> It seemed to charge me with His death
>   Though not a word He spoke.

> My conscience felt and owned my guilt,
>   And plunged me in despair.
> I saw my sins His blood had spilt,
>   And helped to nail Him there.

A second look He gave, which said—
"I freely all forgive:
This blood is for thy ransom paid,
I die that thou may'st live".

What a biography! John Newton, the "wretch", plunging on headlong on his "wild career" had been stopped and mastered; a sight of Christ on the cross had been sufficient.

"All hail, the power of Jesus' name"

Edward Perronet (1726-1792)

South Cloister, Canterbury Cathedral.
(Burial Site of Edward Perronet).

E. P. Scott, a missionary in India, saw in the street one day an obvious stranger. On enquiry as to his identity, he was told that he was a member of a distant inland mountain tribe who had come down to the city to trade. On further enquiry, Scott discovered these mountain people were heathen and had never been reached with the gospel but that to venture among them was very dangerous. The news caused Scott deep exercise of heart. He retired to his lodging, fell on his knees and cried to God in earnest intercession. But before he rose, he felt that God was calling him personally to carry the gospel to them. He packed his few belongings, picked up his violin and pilgrim staff and went to bid farewell to his fellow-missionaries. "We will never see you again", they said, "it is madness for you to go". "But", he replied, "I must carry Jesus to them".

He set out and after some two days of trekking over difficult terrain, located the tribe. Quickly the heathen savages surrounded him, every spear pointing towards his heart. In those tense moments Scott raised his violin, drew upon its strings and with upturned face and closed eyes started to sing,

> *All hail, the power of Jesus' name!*
> *Let angels prostrate fall;*
> *Bring forth the royal diadem,*
> *And crown Him Lord of all.*
>
> *Crown Him, ye martyrs of our God,*
> *Who from His altar call;*
> *Extol the stem of Jesse's rod,*
> *And crown Him Lord of all.*
>
> *Ye chosen seed of Israel's race,*
> *A remnant weak and small;*
> *Hail Him, who saves you by His grace,*
> *And crown Him Lord of all.*
>
> *Ye Gentile sinners, ne'er forget*
> *The wormwood and the gall,*
> *Go, spread your trophies at His feet,*
> *And crown Him Lord of all.*
>
> *Let every kindred, every tribe*
> *On this terrestrial ball,*
> *To Him all majesty ascribe,*
> *And crown Him Lord of all.*

When Scott had reached the verse, "Let every kindred, every tribe", he opened his eyes and, lo, a wonder had taken place. Every spear had dropped from their hands and tears were streaming down their faces. They invited him to their homes and for two and a half years he lived and laboured in their midst. At the end of that period his health had so deteriorated that he decided he must go home. The tribe's people accompanied him for some thirty to forty miles on his journey. "Oh, missionary", they said in parting, "come back to us again. There are tribes beyond us that never heard the glad tidings of salvation". So, after restoration of health, Scott returned to their midst and there he spent the remainder of his days.

The majestic hymn, "All hail, the power of Jesus' name", sung by Scott on that memorable occasion, was written by Edward Perronet some two hundred years ago. Edward Perronet was a descendant of a distinguished Huguenot family who, because of their faith, had suffered much persecution in their native homeland of France. Edward's grandfather, David Perronet, had come to England in 1680. Edward's father, the godly Vincent Perronet, was a minister in the Church of England and for over fifty years was vicar of Shoreham in Kent. He was an earnest evangelical, closely identified with the great revival of the 18th century and an intimate friend of John Wesley. Vincent lived to the ripe age of ninety-one and many were the occasions when John Wesley visited Shoreham on horse-back to spend time with this white-haired and respected saint of God.

Edward Perronet, the subject of this sketch, was born at Sundridge in Kent in 1726. He grew up at Shoreham rectory and there received his early education under a tutor. His upbringing was very much influenced by the traditions of the Church of England and there was every hope that Edward would, one day, become one of its ministers. As a youth, however, he had regarded John Wesley as his hero and, when he became a young man, identified himself with the Wesleys and the Methodist movement. For years, together with his brother Charles, Edward travelled up and down the country in their company and for the cause of the gospel of Christ, suffered much persecution.

The relationship between the Perronets and John Wesley, however, was not always harmonious. By nature Edward was passionate, impulsive, strong-willed and rebellious; besides he was a man of sharp intellect, of deep insight and of a critical mind. With his facile pen he set about to expose the shortcomings of the

Established Church, much to the displeasure of Wesley. Other differences arose and eventually the Perronets and Wesley parted company, Wesley entering in his record that Charles Perronet, "desisted for want of health" and Edward "for some change of opinion".

After rupture with the Methodist movement, Edward Perronet then became minister in one of the Countess of Huntingdon's chapels in Watling Street, Canterbury, but after a brief ministry resigned from that charge to become pastor in a small but strongly evangelical chapel in the same city and there he continued for the remainder of his days. The ambition of his life had been to serve his Lord devotedly and faithfully, and at the close, in dying and yet undying words, he still sought only the glory of God.

> "Glory to God in the height of His divinity;
> Glory to God in the depth of His humanity;
> Glory to God in His all-sufficiency,
> And into His hands I commend my spirit".

Thus Edward Perronet passed away at Canterbury on January 2nd, 1792; he was buried in the cloisters of Canterbury Cathedral.

Edward Perronet was both a poet and a hymn-writer. His works received publication, often anonymously, in the later half of the 18th century; these appeared in several small volumes, as *Select Passages of the Old and New Testament Versified* (1756), *A Small Collection of Hymns, etc., Canterbury* (1782) and *Occasional Verses, Moral and Sacred* (1785).

"All hail, the power of Jesus' name!" is the crowning jewel of all Perronet's compositions. Its popularity now for over two hundred years bears ample testimony to its undoubted worth. It is a hymn that will never die. It first received attention in November, 1779, when its first verse, together with an accompanying tune, "Miles Lane", appeared in *The Gospel Magazine*. Then the completed hymn of eight stanzas, as Perronet had originally penned it, was published in the following April and entitled, "On the Resurrection, the Lord is King". Some years later the hymn was recast by Dr. John Rippon and this is the form in which it appears in most hymnals today. In this modification some of Perronet's original stanzas were omitted, some rewritten and a closing stanza, entirely the work of Dr. Rippon, was added,

> *O that, with yonder sacred throng,*
> *We at His feet may fall;*
> *Join in the everlasting song,*
> *And crown Him Lord of all!*

There is a majesty about this hymn which is unique and nothing thrills the heart more than to hear it well sung by a large congregation to one or other of its companion tunes, either "Miles Lane" or "Diadem". Both these tunes were written by young men while still in their teens—"Miles Lane" by William Shrubsole, a chorister in Canterbury Cathedral, and "Diadem" by James Ellor, a hat-maker from Droylsden village in Lancashire.

The words of this hymn command attention. **"All hail"**—it was the glorious and joyous salutation of the risen Lord on the resurrection morning as He stepped out on the upward pathway to ever-increasing exaltation and glory. Edward Perronet in this hymn anticipates the final movement, majestic and triumphant; as at the first, so on that day, devotion's response will be, "they came and held Him by the feet, and worshipped Him" (Matt. 28:9). **"Crown Him"**—the "crown rights", undisputed, undivided, universal and eternal belong to Jesus Christ; they are His by Sovereign decree and His because of Calvary. His rights still await recognition; when that day comes no dissenting voice will be heard and gladly will we, His redeemed, join in the universal proclamation, "He is Lord of all" (Acts 10:36).

"There is a fountain filled with blood"

William Cowper (1731-1800)

William Cowper.

In the eighteenth century when England was wrapped in gloomy and sullen silence and literary genius seemed dead, the voice of William Cowper heralded a new day. "Cowper", says Macauley, "was the forerunner of the great restoration of our literature". Dr. Arnold terms him, "the singer of the dawn".

William Cowper, the poet, was born in his father's rectory at Berkhampstead, Hertfordshire, on November 15th, 1731. He was

77

a delicate and emotionally sensitive boy. His mother, his one source of comfort, died when he was six and his father, lacking in understanding of the ways of his boy, packed him off to a distant boarding school. There he was bullied and beaten, the object of fun and derision among the boys; his was a childhood of loneliness, fear and insecurity.

At eighteen, William began to study law, but was never mentally equipped to follow such a career. He was called to the Bar in 1754, and later was nominated to the "Clerkship of the Journals" of the House of Lords. The dread of appearing before the House to show his fitness for the appointment overthrew his reason and, as a consequence, he tried to commit suicide. He was then placed under the care of Dr. Nathaniel Cotton and admitted to a small mental home in St. Albans where he remained for almost two years. There he was restored mentally and there he was saved spiritually. He was then thirty years of age.

Let Cowper himself tell of that unforgettable experience: "All that passed during these eight months was conviction of sin and despair of mercy . . . I flung myself into a chair near the window and, seeing a Bible there, ventured once more to apply to it for comfort and instruction. The first verses I saw were in the third of Romans: 'Being justified freely by His grace through the redemption that is in Christ Jesus, whom God has set forth to be a propitiation through faith in His blood, to manifest His righteousness'. Immediately, I received strength to believe and the full beams of the Sun of Righteousness shone upon me. I saw the sufficiency of the atonement He had made, my pardon in His blood, and the fulness and completeness of His justification. In a moment I believed and received the gospel". Rapturous joy filled Cowper's heart. He devoted himself to prayer and thanksgiving and for weeks tears flowed when he thought or spoke of the Saviour.

On discharge from hospital, Cowper moved to Huntingdon but found that he was unable to live alone, "I felt like a traveller in the midst of an inhospitable desert, without a friend to comfort". At that time the acquaintance and hospitality of the Unwin family proved invaluable. He was received into their home and Morley and Mary Unwin cared for him as they would have an adopted son. There he felt at home and was given the care and security that he needed. Mary Unwin proved to be a great stay in Cowper's life.

He referred to her in his later writings as "the chief of blessings I have met with on my journey".

Following Morley's death in 1767, Mrs. Unwin, her daughter and Cowper moved to Olney in Buckinghamshire at the invitation of John Newton. There a close friendship was formed between the two men, even though they differed greatly in personality and temperament. Cowper was shy, sensitive and delicate; Newton, by six years the senior, ever remained the stocky, robust old sea captain. At Olney they lived together in close association and in perfect harmony. Those were the happy days of the Olney prayer-meetings, the days in which the "Olney hymns" were born. (A hymn was composed by either Cowper or Newton for each weekly prayer-meeting. The collected volume numbered about three hundred and fifty, of which some sixty-eight were composed by Cowper.)

However, clouds of depression and despair soon returned and Cowper was again plunged into deep darkness. Thought of final banishment from God continually troubled him but when the end approached, the cloud lifted, his face lit up and he exclaimed, "I am not shut out of Heaven after all". Thus concluded the earthly pilgrimage of William Cowper on April 25th, 1800. His dear friend John Newton conducted his funeral service and his body was laid to rest in the churchyard at East Dereham.

Newton and Cowper had shared intimately in spiritual things. Newton understood his friend as few others had ever done and saw in him a holiness of life which he admired, "I can hardly form an idea of a closer walk with God than he uniformly maintained". In anticipation of the moment of their reunion on the other side, Newton pictured to himself clasping again the hand of his dear friend and addressing him:

> Oh! let thy memory wake! I told thee so;
> I told thee thus would end thy heaviest woe;
> I told thee that thy God would bring thee here,
> And God's own hand would wipe away thy tear,
> While I should claim a mansion at thy side;
> I told thee so—for our Immanuel died.

Cowper's writings, both in verse and in song, are among the richest which we have today in the English language. It has been said that in them, "we are brought face to face with an agony which would have been voiceless but for the mercy and goodness of God". Beattie remarks that, "a hymn is the voice speaking from the soul a few words that often represent a whole life"; so in Cowper's hymns, we listen to the very cry of his soul, at one time upon the mountain-top and at another, out of the deepest depths. It was during the mountain-top days at Olney when enjoying the richness of fellowship with God, that he wrote, "Oh, for a closer walk with God", basing it upon the Scripture text, "Enoch walked with God" (Gen. 5:24). Later, in 1773, when about to be plunged again into the darkness of deep mental and spiritual depression he wrote his immortal hymn, "God moves in a mysterious way", of which Montgomery says that it "was written in the twilight of a departing reason".

"There is a fountain filled with blood" is another of Cowper's great hymns; its words will never die and will be sung as long as there are sinners upon the earth. This hymn was written at Olney and is the history of Cowper's own conversion experience. When almost distracted by the burden of his personal sin, his heart cried out, "Oh, for some fountain open for sin and uncleanness". But how could he find it? When all seemed hopeless, he contemplated relief in a premature death. Even in this he felt guilty of committing the unpardonable sin. Then the light suddenly broke. "There shone upon me the full beam of the sufficiency of the atonement that Christ had made, my pardon in His blood...".

> There is a fountain filled with blood
>   Drawn from Immanuel's veins;
> And sinners, plunged beneath that flood,
>   Lose all their guilty stains.
>
> The dying thief rejoiced to see
>   That fountain in his day;
> And there have I, though vile as he,
>   Washed all my sins away.
>
> Dear, dying Lamb! Thy precious blood
>   Shall never lose its power,
> Till all the ransom'd Church of God
>   Be saved to sin no more.

E'er since, by faith, I saw the stream
Thy flowing wounds supply,
Redeeming love has been my theme
And shall be till I die.

Soon, in a nobler, sweeter song
I'll sing Thy power to save:
When this poor lisping, stammering tongue
Lies silent in the grave.

"The blood of Christ!"—It is the sweetest strain that has ever fallen upon the ear of a sin-stained soul on earth (1 John 1:7).
"The blood of Christ!"—It will be the sweet employ of redeemed hearts through eternal ages (Rev. 1:5).
"The blood of Christ!"—It once filled and flooded the soul of William Cowper and there flowed from his pen the lines of this immortal hymn.

It is good for us to remember, however, that these immortal lines were born out of the experience of one whose life was lived for the most part under a dark cloud, and of whom it has been said: "Divine grace raised his head when he was a companion of lunatics, to make him (by a most mysterious dispensation of gifts) a poet of the highest intellectuality and in song an unshaken, uncompromising confessor of the purest doctrine of the gospel, even when he himself had lost sight of its consolations".

The once storm-tossed soul of William Cowper now rests in a peaceful haven on another shore. The compositions of his pen live on and will never die; and that this is so is beautifully expressed by one who once visited his grave at East Dereham.

I went alone. 'Twas summer-time;
And standing there before the shrine
Of that illustrious bard,
I read his own familiar name,
And thought of his extensive fame,
And felt devotion's sacred flame
Which we do well to guard.

"There is a fountain". As I stood
I thought I saw the crimson "flood"
And some beneath "the wave";
I thought the stream still rolled along,
And that I saw the "ransomed" throng,
And that I heard the "nobler song"
Of Jesus' "power to save".

"O for a closer"—even so,
For we who journey here below
Have lived too far from God.
Oh, for that holy life I said,
Which Enoch, Noah, Cowper, led!
Oh, for that "purer light" to shed
Its brightness on "the road"!

"God moves in a mysterious way";
But now the poet seemed to say,
"No mysteries remain.
On earth I was a sufferer,
In Heaven I am a conqueror;
God is His own interpreter,
And He has made it plain."

"Come Thou Fount of every blessing"

Robert Robinson (1735-1790)

Robert Robinson.

One day, towards the close of the 18th century, a gentleman and lady sat side by side in a stage-coach as it rumbled its way through the English countryside. The lady appeared to be occupied with the content of the book in her hand, at times reading from its open page, at times meditating on what she had just read. She was obviously enjoying her musings, the words of a lovely hymn:

83

Come, Thou Fount of every blessing,
Tune my heart to sing Thy grace;
Streams of mercy, never ceasing,
Call for songs of loudest praise.
Teach me some melodious measure,
Sung by flaming tongues above;
O the vast, the boundless treasure
Of my Lord's unchanging love!

Here I raise mine Ebenezer;
Hither, by Thy help, I'm come;
And I hope by Thy good pleasure,
Safely to arrive at home.
Jesus sought me when a stranger
Wandering from the fold of God;
He, to rescue me from danger,
Interposed His precious blood.

O to grace how great a debtor
Daily I'm constrained to be!
Let the grace, Lord, like a fetter,
Bind my wandering heart to Thee.
Prone to wander, Lord, I feel it,
Prone to leave the God I love;
Take my heart, O take and seal it,
Seal it for Thy courts above.

She turned to the gentleman, to her a stranger, and sought to interest him in what was obviously delighting her heart. Holding before him the open page she enquired if he knew the hymn. At first he appeared embarrassed, even a little agitated; then he tried to parry her question but she persisted, telling him of the blessing that the words had brought to her own heart. After a period of silence, he burst into tears. "Madam", he said, "I am the poor, unhappy man who composed that hymn many years ago, and I would give a thousand worlds, if I had them, to enjoy the feelings I had then". The gentleman on the stage-coach was Robert Robinson; the hymn was the product of his pen some thirty years previously.

Robert Robinson was born of lowly parents at Swaffam, Norfolk, on September 27th, 1735. In his native town he had been a pupil at the "Latin School" and then later in Mildenhall at its Endowed Grammar School where his master pronounced him, "a youth of large capacity, uncommon genius and refined taste". Robert had lost his father when he was eight and thereafter received the devoted care of his widowed mother whose one ambition for her boy was that he might become a clergyman in the Church of England. The circumstances of poverty, however, forbade such a pursuit.

As a youth of fourteen, Robert was apprenticed to a hairdresser in London but this work failed to interest him. He spent most of his time reading books; he was by nature a thoughtful and studious lad. He was besides a wild lad and early in his London days got linked up with a group of ungodly young men who habitually led him into trouble. Indeed, the time came when his deeds so shamed his own family that they refused to be responsible for his liabilities.

Then, at the age of seventeen, an incident happened which completely changed Robert's whole life. The eventful day was May 24th, 1752, when his companions and he joined together to make sport of an old drunken fortune-teller; they wanted to laugh at her predictions. The old lady told Robinson of his future, that he would live to be a very old man and that he would see many generations of descendants. This prediction so impressed Robinson that he reasoned with himself, "and so, I am to see children, grandchildren and great-grandchildren. I will then, during my youth, endeavour to store my mind with all kinds of knowledge. I will see and hear and note down everything that is rare and wonderful, that I may sit, when incapable of other employments, and entertain my descendants. Then shall my company be rendered pleasant and I shall be respected, rather than neglected, in old age. Let me see, what can I acquire first? Oh, here is the famous Methodist preacher, Whitefield; he is to preach here, they say tonight; I will go and hear him".

Robinson went the same evening to the Tabernacle to hear Whitefield who, for that meeting, took as his text Matt. 3:7, "But when he (John the Baptist) saw many of the Pharisees and Sadducees come to his baptism, he said unto them, 'O generation of vipers, who hath warned you to flee from the wrath to come?' ". Mr. Whitefield got to work on his text. He portrayed the Sadducees but his words failed to touch Robinson's heart for he felt himself to be as good as any other. Then Mr. Whitefield described the Pharisees—ostentatious, seemingly righteous but within their hearts was the poisonous venom of the viper. That description fitted his own condition exactly and the word came as an arrow from God, penetrating deep into his heart. He shuddered. The preacher paused and, lifting up his hand to Heaven and with tears flowing down his face, cried as only Mr. Whitefield could, "Oh, my hearers, the wrath to come! the wrath to come!" "Those words", Robinson later recounted to a friend, "sunk into my heart like lead in the water: I wept, and when the sermon was ended retired alone. For days and weeks I could think of little else. Those awful words would follow me wherever I went". Then some three years later, on December 10th, 1755, he "found full and free forgiveness through the precious blood of Jesus Christ". Robinson was then about twenty years of age.

> *Jesus sought me when a stranger*
> *Wandering from the fold of God:*
> *He, to rescue me from danger,*
> *Interposed His precious blood.*

After conversion, Robinson took a deep interest in spiritual things. His heart hungered and thirsted for the Word of God and for about three years he attended whatever meetings he could in the London area. The ministry of Gill and Wesley he found to be particularly satisfying. Robinson became a minister of the gospel, first in his native Norfolk with Calvinistic Methodists at Mildenhall, then for a short period with an Independent congregation at Norwich, and in 1759 he moved to the Baptist Church in Cambridge. The latter was Robinson's most notable ministry.

By 1790, Robinson was worn out and he retired to Birmingham where he passed away on June 9th, 1790, at the age of fifty-five. He was found dead in bed. Earlier he had expressed the wish that he might die, "softly, suddenly and alone"; his wish had been granted to him.

Robinson was an interesting personality; his characteristics were very diverse—sincere but unstable as water, able but most impulsive, eccentric though all the while a genius. As a preacher he had extraordinary talent; audiences were held spellbound under his ministry. As a writer he exhibited considerable ability, an able theologian with upwards of thirty publications coming from his pen; his works on the Person of Christ, of His divinity and His death, merited and received the highest acclaim. As a hymn-writer, Robinson wrote some good hymns, a number of them for children; his compositions on the whole were well wrought and judged by critics as, "terse yet melodious, evangelical but not sentimental".

"Come, Thou Fount of every blessing" is Robinson's best known hymn. It was written early in his Christian experience, around the year 1758. He was then about twenty-three years of age. At that time, he was a young minister in his native Norfolk but in heart was away from the Lord. What was he to do? Should he continue or, in all honesty, should he abandon the Christian ministry? He decided on the latter. Then the words of Psalm 116:7 were directed to his heart, "Return unto thy rest, O my soul; for the LORD hath dealt bountifully with thee". An inner struggle ensued and raged until at last his soul "returned to its rest" and he consecrated himself afresh to the Lord. Afterwards, feeling that a record of his experience might be of help to others, he wrote the lines of this hymn. Subsequent history, however, reveals that in later years he again wandered away in heart from the Lord. He was "prone to wander"; he was "prone to leave". The record tells us though that in life's eventide, he experienced, as aforetime, the restoring grace of God.

We are all "prone to wander", "prone to leave" the God we love. The bent of the human heart is ever to stray from the pathway of fellowship with God, but over against every human departure and every human wandering there is corresponding and sufficient restoring grace; of that Divine grace we all, like Robert Robinson, stand in daily need and to that same grace, we all are daily debtors.

"Come, let us sing the matchless worth"

Samuel Medley (1738-1799)

Samuel Medley.

One Lord's day in October, 1975, a company of believers gathered in a small room in Jerusalem to remember the Lord Jesus. For most it was a first experience in that city—only a few had previously met in that room. Yet for all it was an unforgettable meeting, when for a time the conditions of earth seemed to pass away and the presence of the risen Lord filled and stilled every heart. With tear-dimmed eye and broken voice they sang together:

Come, let us sing the matchless worth,
And sweetly sound the glories forth
Which in the Saviour shine:
To God and Christ our praises bring;
The song, with which the heavens ring,
Now let us gladly join.

How rich the precious blood He spilt,
Our ransom from the dreadful guilt
Of sin against our God.
How perfect is His righteousness,
In which unspotted beauteous dress
His saints have always stood!

Great are the offices He bears,
And bright His character appears,
Exalted on the throne;
In songs of sweet untiring praise,
We would, to everlasting days,
Make all His glories known.

Samuel Medley was the author of this lovely hymn. He was born of godly parents in Cheshunt, Hertfordshire, England, on June 23rd, 1738, and as a lad received education from his grandfather, William Tonge. When he was fourteen, he was apprenticed to an oilman in the city of London; after three years in that trade, he entered the British Navy.

At that time, England was at war and during an engagement with the French enemy off Cape Lagos, Medley received a serious leg injury. Over the succeeding days his leg condition deteriorated and life was endangered. "I am afraid that amputation is the only thing that will save your life", advised the ship's surgeon. "I can tell tomorrow morning". Those words troubled Medley greatly. He appreciated the seriousness of the hour. He had led a profligate life and was not prepared to die. That night he gave himself to prayer that God would restore his leg and preserve his life. Remembering that he had a Bible, he sent his servant to fetch it and throughout the night read it with avidity. God answered his prayer and by the following morning, to the great surprise of the surgeon, his leg had improved dramatically. With the immediate crisis now past, Medley turned again to his old ways and tried to forget about God. His injury, however, had necessitated that he retire from active service; he returned home and came once again under the influence of his godly grandfather. He was then twenty-one years of age.

Grandfather Tonge spoke to him of his ways and of his need of salvation, and on an unforgettable Sunday evening read to him a sermon of Dr. Isaac Watts, based on Isaiah 42:6, 7. That message brought deep conviction of sin and of guilt to Medley's heart, for those words, the words of Dr. Watts' text, "to open the blind eyes, to bring out the prisoners from the prison", seemed so accurately to describe his own heart's condition and need. He sought salvation and found it in Christ, or to use his own words, "I soon received the comforts of the gospel, by a believing view of the fullness and sufficiency of the atonement of the Lord Jesus".

Seven years after conversion, Medley was called to the work as a minister of the gospel. The first five years were spent at Watford and then in 1772, he moved to Byrom Street in the city of Liverpool. There, until God called him 'home' twenty-seven years later, he faithfully and fruitfully preached the glorious gospel to an ever-increasing congregation. There the burden of his ministry was "to humble the pride of man, exalt the grace of God in his salvation and promote real holiness in heart and life". There many a profligate seaman of that city port turned into his meetings and many were blessed eternally. Medley loved those men for he himself had once been as one of them. He understood them as few others could and his heart's sympathy went out to them, right to the close of life. As his hour of death approached, he was heard to say, "I am now a poor shattered bark, just about to gain the blissful harbour; and oh, how sweet will be the port after the storm! . . . but a point or two more, and I shall be in my heavenly Father's house!" Peacefully and triumphantly, on July 17th, 1799, he gained that blissful harbour.

Medley was possessed of an eccentric personality and a poetic turn of mind, making him original in his way. Once, when asked to complete a circular about his church work in Liverpool, he worded his reply as follows:

Q. In what town is your church?

> *In one where sin makes many a fool*
> *Known by the name of Liverpool.*

Q. What is your Christian and surname, degree?

> *My Christian name is called Saint,*
> *My surname rather odd and quaint,*
> *But to explain the whole with ease,*
> *Saint Samuel Medley, if you please;*
> *And you from hence may plainly see*
> *That I have taken a degree!*

Q. Have you an assistant?

> *O yes! I've One of whom I boast*
> *His name is called the Holy Ghost.*

Q. What number of people attend?

> *A many come, my worthy friend,*
> *I dare not say they all attend;*
> *But though so many, great and small,*
> *I never number them at all,*
> *For that was once poor David's fall.*

As a hymn-writer, Medley wrote over two hundred hymns. Many of these were originally written on broadsheets for distribution and after his death were published collectively in book form. In writing verse, Medley's deep desire was the glory of Christ and the comfort of the people of God. A sense of deep gratitude to God for personal salvation ever filled his heart and found expression in verse in some of his hymns as, "Awake my soul, in joyful lays" ("His loving-kindness") and "Now, in a song of grateful praise" ("My Jesus has done all things well").

Medley's hymn, "Come, let us sing the matchless worth" has been greatly modified with the passing of the years and as a result has lost some of the original pathos with which it first came from the pen of Liverpool's illustrious hymn-writer. In its original the hymn's opening stanza ran thus:

O, could I speak the matchless worth,
O, could I sound the glories forth,
  Which in my Saviour shine!
I'd soar and touch the heavenly strings,
And vie with Gabriel while he sings,
  In notes almost divine.

Medley's heart was occupied with his Saviour. His subject matter was great—His matchless worth! His precious blood! His perfect righteousness! His manifold ministries!—and the rich verse coming from his pen was but the overflow of a full heart. Truly in this, he shared in the experience of the Psalmist, "My heart is welling forth with a good matter: I say what I have composed touching the king . . . fairer than the sons of men" (Psa. 45:1, 2, J.N.D.).

"Rock of Ages"

Augustus Montague Toplady (1740-1778)

Augustus Montague Toplady.

"Rock of Ages", written over two hundred years ago by Augustus Montague Toplady when in his early twenties, is a great hymn and has found its way into millions of hearts. Dr. John Julian says of it, "No other English hymn can be named that has laid so broad and firm a grasp upon the English-speaking world". "Rock of Ages" has also been translated into many other languages. Dr. Pomeroy once found himself in an Armenian church in Constantinople. The worshippers there were singing but he could

not understand their language. Nevertheless he discerned the
effect; their hearts were stirred and tears were streaming down
many of their faces. When he enquired as to the meaning of the
words which they sang, he learned that it was the Arabic
translation of "Rock of Ages".

Augustus Montague Toplady was born on November 14th,
1740, at Farnham in Surrey, England. When he was only a few
months old he lost his father at the siege of Cartagena; thereafter
he was cared for by his widowed mother. Augustus was sent to
Westminster School for his early education and then, through
force of circumstance and yet in the providence of God, his
mother and he moved to Ireland. There, at Trinity College,
Dublin, he received further education and while in Ireland he was
saved by the grace of God.

It happened thus that Augustus, then a lad of sixteen, was
travelling one evening with his mother in County Wexford when
they overheard singing coming from a barn. They stopped to listen
and then ventured to enter. When the singing was over a simple
humble servant of God, named James Morris, ministered fervently
from the Scripture text, "Ye who sometimes were afar off are
made nigh by the blood of Christ" (Eph. 2:13). On that night and
under those words young Augustus Montague Toplady was
brought nigh to God by the blood of Christ. "Strange", he
afterwards recounted, "that I who had so long sat under the means
of grace in England, should be brought nigh unto God in an
obscure part of Ireland midst a handful of people met together in a
barn, and by the ministry of one who could scarcely spell his own
name. Surely it was the Lord's doing and is marvellous".

Toplady graduated M.A. from Trinity College in 1760 and in
the following year was ordained a minister in the Church of
England. His first charge was as curate at Blagdon in Somerset and
there he spent two years. Then, following two further brief
curacies, he was appointed vicar of Broadhembury in Devon in
1768. After a ministry there of some seven years his health started
to fail and he moved to London. In the English capital he found the
atmosphere more congenial and his friends acquired for him the
use of the Chapel of the French Calvinists in Leicester Fields;
there, for a period of two years he preached the gospel regularly to
large congregations of some twelve to fifteen hundred people.

Toplady, as a preacher, was both magnetic and lucid—"such

commanding solemnity in his tones as made apathy impossible, and such simplicity in his words that to hear was to understand. He was an outspoken Calvinist and impulsive in his manner, yet a man of deep piety. He yearned after personal holiness and consecrated all his intellectual gift and learning unto the Lord.

Throughout life, Toplady enjoyed the assurance of personal salvation in Christ and termed himself "the happiest man in the world". He maintained a triumphant spirit right to the close and in his final illness, when the doctor indicated that his pulse was weakening, he rejoiced, "Why, that is a good sign that my death is fast approaching; and, blessed be God, I can add that my heart beats every day stronger and stronger for glory". Then on August 11th, 1778, as he awaited his Lord's final call, he burst into tears of joy exclaiming, "It will not be long before God takes me, for no mortal can live after the glories which God has manifested to my soul". Thus, in his thirty-eighth year, Augustus Montague Toplady passed away to glory.

Toplady, in his lifetime, wrote a number of hymns and of these many were good hymns and greatly used of the Lord. The words of his, "A debtor to mercy alone" and of his, "From whence this fear and unbelief" have often been used to dispel perplexity of doubt from the heart and establish in its place the calm assurance of salvation. "Rock of Ages", however, has been acclaimed beyond all else that has come from his pen and it is as author of this one hymn that Toplady is remembered today; an interesting story has often been linked with its writing:

Toplady at that time was curate-in-charge of the parish of Blagdon in Somerset. One day he was overtaken by a severe thunder-storm in Burrington Combe, a rocky glen which runs up into the Mendip Hills. There was no habitation near at hand and so he took refuge between two massive pillars of rock; the precipitous limestone crag there, towering one hundred feet high, had been split right down its centre by a deep cleft or fissure. As he sheltered from the fury of the thunder-storm in that natural refuge, his mind turned to his spiritual refuge in the Lord Jesus, the true "Rock of Ages" (Isa. 26:4—marginal reading) and with such thought in his mind there flowed from his pen words which were to become immortal.

Rock of Ages, cleft for me,
Let me hide myself in Thee!
Let the water and the blood,
From Thy riven side which flow'd,
Be of sin the double cure,
Cleanse me from its guilt and pow'r.

Not the labour of my hands
Can fulfil Thy law's demands;
Could my zeal no respite know,
Could my tears for ever flow,
All for sin could not atone:
Thou must save, and Thou alone!

Nothing in my hand I bring,
Simply to Thy cross I cling;
Naked, come to Thee for dress;
Helpless, look to Thee for grace;
Foul, I to the fountain fly;
Wash me, Saviour, or I die!

Whilst I draw this fleeting breath—
When my eye-strings break in death—
When I soar through tracts unknown—
See Thee on Thy judgment-throne—
Rock of Ages, cleft for me,
Let me hide myself in Thee!

These words first appeared in *The Gospel Magazine* (March 1776) and were entitled, "A living and dying Prayer for the Holiest Believer in the World". Many, through the years, have found them to be so. Prince Albert, the Prince Consort, asked for them and quoted them in his dying moments, "Rock of Ages, cleft for me, let me hide myself in Thee". "For", he added, "if in this hour, I had only my worldly honours and dignities to depend on, I should be poor indeed". Nor are these words only for the noble and rich. They meet the need of every storm-tossed soul, directing each away from personal toil, personal attainment, personal zeal and even tears of contrition to Christ alone for salvation.

"Stricken, smitten, and afflicted"

Thomas Kelly (1769-1854)

Monument to Thomas Kelly.
Ballintubbert, near to Kellyville, Co. Laoise, Ireland.

Thomas Kelly is probably Ireland's greatest and most prolific hymn-writer. The only son of Judge Thomas Kelly of Kellyville, Queen's County, Ireland, he was born in the city of Dublin on July 13th, 1769. Judge Kelly intended for his son a career at the Bar, and so, after graduating with honours from Trinity College, Dublin, Thomas entered the Temple, in London. While studying there and while yet in his early twenties, he was converted to God. He had been using Romaine's edition of *Colosio's Hebrew Concordance* and his enquiring mind had led him to a deeper perusal of Romaine's evangelical doctrines. That pursuit produced within his heart a deep conviction of sin and of his true state before God. Earnestly desiring Divine approval, he diligently sought to obtain it through his own merit and only when self-reformation, fasting and other forms of practical asceticism had all proved futile, he found salvation and peace through believing in the Lord Jesus Christ.

At the age of twenty-three, he left the Bar and returned to Ireland where he was ordained a minister of the Established Church. However, Kelly was too fervent and forceful a preacher of justification by faith alone to be allowed to stay within the Established Church. He incurred the displeasure of Archbishop Fowler of Dublin who, thereupon, closed to him all the pulpits of the diocese. Thus debarred from consecrated buildings, Kelly moved outside the Established Church and crowds flocked to hear him, attracted by his magnetic presence. A writer of those times stated that, "his presence, his conversation, his learning were all tending to improve his intercourse with others; for they felt that they were enjoying the society of one who was 'on his way to God'". Nevertheless, he had to withstand bitter opposition in those days and especially from members of his own family. This caused him much heartbreak for he felt that in many ways it would have been easier to have died at the stake than to have gone against his family.

The subsequent years of Kelly's life were spent around the city of Dublin and all of those years were full for God. As a man of influence and means, he became "a friend of good men" and "an advocate of every worthy cause". Possessed of a gracious and generous spirit, his liberality was acknowledged by all and he was greatly beloved among the poor of Dublin city, particularly so in the days of the potato famine in the 1840's. He became renowned as one of Ireland's finest evangelical preachers, as one of her greatest scholars and as one of her most distinguished spiritual poets. Singleness of purpose marked all his earthly way, right till its close on May 14th, 1854, and one has written over those sixty-three years of busy ministry, "his language, his temper, his recreations, as well as his serious studies, were all regulated by the same rule, to do all to the glory of God".

Thomas Kelly, "the hymnist of Ireland", has left for us a rich treasury in verse. His compositions were the simple and natural expression of an overflowing heart. His subject was the Word of God and his poetical works were published as such, *Hymns on Various Passages of Scripture.* Its first edition, published in 1804, contained ninety-six of his hymns, and its tenth edition, published in 1853 (the year preceding his death), contained seven hundred and sixty-five of his hymns. In the preface of this last edition Kelly wrote, "It will be perceived by those who have read these hymns that, though there is an interval between the first and the last of nearly fifty years, both speak of the same great truths and in the same way. In the course of that long time the author has seen much and heard much, but nothing has made the least change in his mind that he is conscious of as to the grand truths of the gospel. What pacified the conscience then does so now. What gave hope then does so now. 'Other foundation can no man lay than that is laid, which is Christ Jesus' ".

When Kelly took up his pen, the person and work of the Lord Jesus was his compelling theme—Christ's cross and His resurrection, Christ's exaltation and priestly ministry, Christ's second advent and His coming glory: on these majestic themes probably no nobler verse can anywhere be found. His hymns rank among the first in the English language, lifting high the person of the Lord Jesus while, at the same time, bowing low the heart in worship and calling forth the heart to praise. Besides his poetic distinction, Kelly was an accomplished musician and composer, compiling a companion volume of music to his *Hymns on Various Passages of Scripture.*

Kelly's store is vast. The following serve to illustrate something of the richness, the beauty and the grandeur that marked his compositions:

> "Behold the Lamb with glory crowned"
> "Crowns of glory ever bright"
> "Glory, glory everlasting"
> "Glory to God on high"
> "God is love, His word has said it"
> "Look, ye saints, the sight is glorious"
> "Meeting in the Saviour's Name"
> "Praise the Lord who died to save us"
> "Praise the Saviour, ye who know Him"

"Saviour, through the desert lead us"
"Stricken, smitten, and afflicted"
"The atoning work is done"
"The head that once was crowned with thorns"
"We sing the praise of Him who died"
"We'll sing of the Shepherd that died"
"Without blood is no remission"

In those privileged and precious moments at the Lord's Supper, the believer's carnal and wandering thoughts have oftimes been elevated and stayed by some phrase or line from Kelly's pen. Likewise, in gospel testimony, Kelly fixes and enlarges our view of the grand truths of the gospel,

> Stricken, smitten and afflicted,
>   See Him dying on the tree!
> 'Tis the Christ by man rejected,
>   Yes, my soul, 'tis He! 'tis He!
> Many hands were raised to wound Him,
>   None would interpose to save;
> But the awful stroke that found Him
>   Was the stroke that justice gave.
>
> Ye who think of sin but lightly,
>   Nor suppose the evil great,
> Here may view its nature rightly,
>   Here its guilt may estimate.
> Mark the sacrifice appointed!
>   See who bears the awful load!
> 'Tis the Word, the Lord's Anointed
>   Son of Man, and Son of God.
>
> Here we have a firm foundation,
>   Here's the refuge of the lost;
> Christ the Rock of our salvation;
>   His the Name of which we boast.
> Lamb of God, for sinners wounded
>   Sacrificed to cancel guilt!
> None shall ever be confounded
>   Who on Him their hopes have built.

What a picture unfolds as Kelly introduces the Saviour! The magnificence of the One who interposes to save is enhanced by the dark background of the sinner's awesome plight. We watch with deep intent—the One appointed of God and anointed of God intervenes on the sinner's behalf, is "stricken, smitten, and afflicted". Justice is fully and for ever satisfied, for there is no mitigation of sentence at Calvary. This indeed, and this alone is the sinner's refuge, his only hope.

"For ever with the Lord"

James Montgomery (1771-1854)

James Montgomery.

James Montgomery was born in Irvine, Ayrshire, Scotland, on November 4th, 1771. He was the son of a Moravian minister who had earlier been an Irish peasant, and when James was five years of age his parents moved back to Ireland to the Moravian settlement at Gracehill near to Ballymena. At the age of seven James was sent to Fulneck Seminary near to Leeds in Yorkshire to study for the Moravian ministry. He remained there for nine to ten years and during this period his parents left as missionaries to the West

Indies where they both died, one in Barbados and the other in Tobago. James' record at Fulneck Seminary was a great disappointment; in fact, one writer records that he was "distinguished only by indolence and melancholy". He was a daydreamer, a visionary, more interested in making poetry than in his lessons. His school record at Fulneck concluded with the entry, "James Montgomery, notwithstanding repeated admonitions, has not been more attentive. It was resolved to put him to a business, at least for a time".

At the age of sixteen, James was apprenticed to a baker. In this too he showed little interest and the years that followed were marked by restlessness and frequent changes of employment throughout Yorkshire. He was a born poet and during these years he continued to write verse. He sought for a publisher for his youthful compositions and with this in mind travelled as far as London, but his journey there was in vain and he returned to Yorkshire a very disappointed young man.

When he was twenty-one, he applied successfully for a post in Sheffield as assistant to Mr. Joseph Gales who was editor and printer of the *Sheffield Register*. After two years Mr. Gales was forced to leave England to avoid prosecution by the authorities for some publications in his paper which were regarded as "seditious and revolutionary". Thereupon, James Montgomery took over the newspaper, changed its name to the *Sheffield Iris* and continued as its editor and publisher for the next thirty-one years. He was fined and imprisoned for "unpopular" publishing on two occasions, the first for reprinting a song on "The Fall of the Bastille" and the second for criticising the action of a magistrate in dispersing a riot in Sheffield. But "dungeons cannot hold the soul" and in the prison cell Montgomery continued to write verse. (*Prison Amusements* was published in 1797.)

James Montgomery never married. For many years he lived at the *Iris* office in central Sheffield, but in later life moved to the famous "Mount" at the west-end of the city and there continued to write his hymns and poems. In the public life of the city he played a large part and was very highly respected; his fellow townsmen recognized that "his life and his hymns had one music". Indeed, such was his recognised leadership in civic life that at the age of sixty-four he was awarded a National Pension by Sir Robert Peel. He was a pioneer in many humanitarian enterprises, an active denunciator of the slave trade and a great advocate of missionary work, the Bible Society and Sunday-schools. When, at the age of eighty-two, he passed away peacefully at the "Mount" on April 30th, 1854, he was honoured by a public funeral and in the city of Sheffield there are to his memory, a Wesleyan Chapel, a public hall, a statue in the general cemetery and a stained glass window in the parish church.

James Montgomery was a deeply spiritual man but it was not, however, till the age of forty-three that he received a definite assurance of his salvation. Until then he knew no true rest for his heart and confessed in writing to a friend, "What can I do? I am tossed to and fro on a sea of doubts and perplexities; the further I am carried from that shore where I was once happily moored, the weaker grow my hopes of ever reaching another where I may anchor in safety". On knowing the peace of assurance he joined himself to the fellowship of the Moravian brethren, though for most of his time in Sheffield he worshipped with the Methodists because there was no Moravian church there.

James Montgomery, as a poet and hymn-writer, has outstanding merit. As a poet, Lord Byron wrote of him as, "a man of considerable genius". As a hymn-writer, Hugh Martin termed him, "the layman who left an imperishable inheritance". Dr. Routley called him, "the greatest of Christian lay hymn-writers". Dr. Julian says of Montgomery, "the secrets of his power as a writer of hymns were manifold. His poetic genius was of a high order, higher than most who stood with him in the front rank of Christian poets. His ear for rhythm was exceedingly accurate and refined. His knowledge of Holy Scripture was most extensive. His religious views were broad and charitable. His devotional spirit was of the holiest type. With the faith of a strong man he united the beauty and simplicity of a child. Richly poetic without exuberance, dogmatic without uncharitableness, tender without sentimentality, elaborate without diffusiveness, richly musical without apparent effort, he has bequeathed the Church of Christ wealth which could only have come from a true genius and a sanctified heart".

James Montgomery's hymns were, on his own confession, "the most serious work of my long life" and number about four hundred. Many of these are still in regular use today. His hymn, "According to Thy gracious Word" is among those most frequently sung by saints gathered at the Lord's supper. Of his hymn, "Prayer is the soul's sincere desire", Montgomery in his lifetime received more messages as to its helpfulness than about anything else he had ever written. But, perhaps, one of the greatest comforts to the hearts of the Lord's people in times of bereavement has been the assuring words of his, "For ever with the Lord!"

The occasion of its writing was in the year 1835. Montgomery had just lost a very close friend in death and had followed him to the grave. Then in his mind there seemed to spring to life a seed which had been planted in childhood at Fulneck when his schoolmaster read some striking passages from "The Grave", a poem by Blair. **"Was the grave the end?"** He turned to his New Testament for consolation and for help, to 1 Thess. 4:16, 17, "For the Lord Himself shall descend from Heaven with a shout, with the voice of the archangel, and with the trump of God: and the dead in Christ shall rise first; then we which are alive and remain shall be caught up together with them in the clouds, to meet the Lord in the air: and so shall we ever be with the Lord". **"No",** he concluded, **"the grave is definitely not the end",** and some days later, he wrote his great hymn of consolation and hope, "For ever with the Lord!" It contained in its original twenty-two stanzas of four lines each and was entitled, "At home in Heaven, I Thess. 4:17".

"For ever with the Lord!"
  Amen, so let it be;
Life from the dead is in that word,
  'Tis immortality.

Here in the body pent,
  Absent from Him I roam,
Yet nightly pitch my moving tent
  A day's march nearer home.

My Father's house on high,
  Home of my soul, how near
At times to faith's foreseeing eye
  Thy golden gates appear!

Ah! then my spirit faints
  To reach the land I love,
The bright inheritance of saints,
  Jerusalem above.

"For ever with the Lord!"
  Father, if 'tis Thy will,
The promise of that faithful word
  E'en here to me fulfil.

Be Thou at my right hand,
  Then can I never fail;
Uphold Thou me, and I shall stand;
  Fight, and I must prevail.

So when my latest breath
  Shall rend the veil in twain,
By death I shall escape from death
  And life eternal gain.

Knowing as I am known,
  How shall I love that word,
And oft repeat before the throne,
  "For ever with the Lord!"

"For ever with the Lord!" It is an assuring and comforting word. Its anticipation quickens the hearts of saints below; its realization satisfies the hearts of saints above.

"From Greenland's icy mountains"

Reginald Heber (1783-1826)

Reginald Heber.

This great missionary hymn was written by Reginald Heber in
the year 1819. Heber was born on April 21st, 1783, into a wealthy
and cultured family at Malpas in Cheshire, England; there his
father was a clergyman in the Church of England. From childhood,
Reginald demonstrated a great love for books and an aptitude for
writing verse; indeed, his elder brother once remarked, "Reginald
doesn't read books, he devours them". After early education at
Whitchurch and Neasden, Reginald entered Brasenose College,

Oxford, at the age of seventeen. There he followed a very distinguished literary career; besides numerous prizes, he carried off what was, at that time, the most coveted award in English literature (the Newdigate Prize) with his famous poem, "Palestine". A Fellowship from the College enabled him, over the next two years, to travel widely throughout Scandinavia, Eastern Europe and Russia; on his return he entered the ministry of the Church of England.

Heber began to preach in Hodnet in 1807 and there in that little Shropshire village he exercised a diligent and devoted ministry which lasted for sixteen years. No less a person than Thackeray has paid fitting tribute to those Hodnet years, ". . . counselling the people in their troubles, advising them in their difficulties, comforting them in their distress, kneeling often at their sick beds at the hazard of his own health, exhorting, encouraging where there was need; where there was strife, the peace-maker; where there was want, the free-giver", and yet throughout all of those demanding and busy years, there burned within Heber's heart a very deep interest in overseas missionary work. In early youth his soul had been fired by the reading of *The Life of Henry Martyn*. Martyn's heroic labours throughout India, his undaunted zeal and martyr's death, had kindled within him an inextinguishable flame, a flame that was soon to consume all his soul's energies.

In the year 1823, the bishopric of Calcutta was offered to Heber with a charge of responsibility, not only for the whole of India, but also for Ceylon and most of the South Pacific. Though this appeared as the fulfilment of a life-long desire, Heber only accepted the charge after deep exercise of heart. "I prayed to God to show me the path of duty and to give me grace to follow it; and the tranquility of mind which I now feel induces me to hope that I have His blessing and approbation". His acceptance opened to him a completely new sphere of service and he was then forty years of age.

Heber gave himself unstintingly to the work—to the preaching of the gospel, the teaching of new converts and the founding of schools throughout that great sub-continent. God blessed bountifully and when fruit appeared Heber's heart rejoiced. At a Tamil service in Tangore, which was attended by thirteen hundred native Christians, he was greatly moved as he heard so many, but lately rescued from the pollution of their heathen idolatry, join to sing the praises of their Redeemer. "For the last ten years, I have longed to witness a scene like this, but the reality exceeds all my expectation. Gladly would I exchange years of common life for one such day as this". Thus it was to be and after only three years of engagement for God in that difficult tropical climate, Heber laid down his sword. On the evening of April 3rd, 1826, having addressed a large company of new converts at Trichinopoly in which he spoke to them of the evils of the caste system, he was suddenly and unexpectedly called to his rest. Thus closed the brief but unforgettable missionary ministry of Reginald Heber concerning which Dr. John Julian has commented, "no memory of Indian annals is holier than that of the three years of ceaseless travel, splendid administration and saintly enthusiasm".

As a hymn-writer, Reginald Heber has gained a place of honour. He composed fifty-seven hymns and these all were written during the Hodnet period of his ministry. Heber, being a man of rare refinement and deep spirituality, desired that hymns sung in church be worthy of Divine service. A need for such hymns existed and he set to work. His compositions soon began to appear in the *Christian Observer*. He compiled a manuscript collection of these together with some by his close friend, Professor H. H. Milman, and some by others, with a view to introducing them into the regular services of the Church of England. His exercise, however, was thwarted by the hierarchy of the church and not until after his death did the content of his manuscript collection receive publication (*Hymns Written and Adapted to the Weekly Church Service of the year*—1827).

There are two of Reginald Heber's compositions that will never die—his majestic adoration hymn, "Holy, holy, holy, Lord God Almighty" and his great missionary hymn, "From Greenland's icy mountains". The latter was written by Heber four years prior to his call to Calcutta and the circumstances of its writing are most interesting. On the Saturday morning preceding Whit Sunday, 1819, he was gathered with some friends around the table in the library of Wrexham vicarage, the home of his father-in-law, Dr. Shipley. Dr. Shipley, at the time Rector of Wrexham and Dean of St. Asaph's, was nominated to preach a sermon the following morning in the parish church in aid of the "Society for the Propagation of the Gospel in Foreign Parts". The Dean requested of Heber, his son-in-law, that he "write something for us to sing at

the morning service". Heber thereupon retired from the table to a
quiet corner of the library. After a short time, Shipley enquired,
"and what have you written?", to which Heber responded:

> From Greenland's icy mountains,
>   From India's coral strand,
> Where Afric's sunny fountains
>   Roll down their golden sand;
> From many an ancient river,
>   From many a palmy plain,
> They call us to deliver
>   Their land from error's chain.
>
> What though the spicy breezes
>   Blow soft o'er Ceylon's isle;
> Though every prospect pleases,
>   And only man is vile;
> In vain with lavish kindness
>   The gifts of God are strown;
> The heathen, in his blindness,
>   Bows down to wood and stone!
>
> Can we, whose souls are lighted
>   With wisdom from on high,
> Can we, to men benighted
>   The lamp of life deny?
> Salvation! yea, salvation!
>   The joyful sound proclaim,
> Till each remotest nation
>   Has learned Messiah's name.

"There, that will do", exclaimed Shipley. "No, no", remarked
Heber, "the sense is not complete", and went on to add a fourth
verse,

> Waft, waft, ye winds, His story;
>   And you, ye waters roll,
> Till, like a sea of glory,
>   It spreads from pole to pole!

> *Till o'er our ransomed nature,*
> *The Lamb for sinner's slain,*
> *Redeemer, King, Creator,*
> *In bliss returns to reign!*

In all, the composition took about twenty minutes and though written on the inspiration of the moment, he did not alter it in any way except for a single word change in verse two from "savage" to "heathen". On the next morning, Whit Sunday, 1819, it was sung for the first time by the congregation of Wrexham Parish Church to an old ballad tune suggested by Heber himself. Its present tune, "Missionary Hymn" was composed just a few years later by Lowell Mason in Savannah, Georgia, U.S.A., and like the writing of the hymn, this fitting tune was also composed on impulse and completed in thirty minutes.

Heber's great missionary hymn makes an arresting appeal to our hearts. Its language is vivid, its scenes so rapidly changing. In it we picture the heathen of every clime and nation, enslaved in their idolatry, bowing down to wood and stone. We can hear them as they call, "Come over... and help us" (Acts 16:9). Their call is not merely that of slaves in their chains, nor of the hungry in their distress, nor even of the sick and suffering in their physical need. It is the call of lost souls, the cry from hearts wrung by the tyranny of sin. It is incessant! It cannot be stifled! It will not go away!

> *Can we, whose souls are lighted*
> *With wisdom from on high,*
> *Can we, to men benighted*
> *The lamp of life deny?*
> *Salvation! yea, salvation!*
> *The joyful sound proclaim,*
> *Till each remotest nation*
> *Has learned Messiah's name.*

"Just as I am"

Charlotte Elliott (1789-1871)

Charlotte Elliott.

Charlotte Elliott, the writer of this well-loved hymn, was born at Clapham on the outskirts of London in 1789, the year of the French Revolution. Clapham, at that period, was the home of many noble statesmen who were Christians. Among them were William Wilberforce, the great pioneer for the abolition of slavery, and Lord Teignmouth the governor of India. These were all members of the National Church and sat under the ministry of the venerable John Venn, their godly vicar. Venn's ministry, however, left Charlotte cold and unmoved; it failed to reach her heart. Yet she demonstrated no antipathy to it, just apathy; as yet she did not personally know the Saviour.

When Charlotte entered her thirties she became greatly concerned about her spiritual state. Her sister tells us that, "she became deeply conscious of the evil of her own heart, and having not yet fully realized the fullness and freeness of the grace of God in the Lord Jesus Christ, she suffered much mental distress under the painful uncertainty whether it were possible that such a one as she felt herself to be could be saved".

The great experience of salvation became a reality for Charlotte in the year 1822. She was then thirty-three years of age. There came at that time to stay at "Grove House", their Clapham home, a distinguished guest from Geneva, Switzerland, whose name was Dr. Caesar Malan. One day that godly man ventured to speak to Charlotte regarding her spiritual state. "Are you a Christian?" he enquired, to which she retorted, "Mind your own business", and left the room. She could not, however, dismiss that question, "Was she a Christian?", and two weeks later, when they were together in the garden, she apologized for her rudeness and confessed to Dr. Malan, "I should like to come to Christ but I don't know how". "My dear young lady", he replied, "you don't want to worry any more about that, come just as you are". Those words of Dr. Caesar Malan to Charlotte that day in the garden, led not only to the birth of a soul but as well to the birth of a song. Dr. Malan wrote to Charlotte on his return to Geneva. Aware of her spiritual struggle and crisis, he tried to encourage her in taking that step to Christ, "One look, silent, but continuous and faithful at the Cross of Jesus is better, is more efficacious than all else beside. Dear Charlotte, cut the cable, it will take too long to unloose it; cut it, it is a small loss, the wind blows and the ocean is before—the Spirit of God and eternity". Charlotte took that step to Christ, that step from the darkness of doubt to the peace and blessedness of eternal light.

It was twelve years later when Charlotte wrote the hymn. She was then living in Brighton with her vicar brother, Henry Venn Elliott, who ran a girls' school there. One evening, when all the others had gone out to a public function, Charlotte was alone at "Westfield Lodge". As she lay that evening on the sofa, feeling downcast and full of doubts and fears, the experience of twelve years earlier and the words of Dr. Caesar Malan again flooded her soul. It took her back to the starting point, to those words that first brought peace to her troubled heart. As she afresh laid hold of those eternal certainties, she felt that she must give expression to her thoughts and, reaching for a pen, she put into verse what had been her own experience.

> *Just as I am—without one plea,*
>   *But that Thy blood was shed for me,*
> *And that Thou bidd'st me come to Thee—*
>   *O Lamb of God, I come!*
>
> *Just as I am—and waiting not*
>   *To rid my soul of one dark blot,*
> *To Thee, whose blood can cleanse each spot—*
>   *O Lamb of God, I come!*
>
> *Just as I am—though tossed about*
>   *With many a conflict, many a doubt,*
> *Fightings and fears, within, without—*
>   *O Lamb of God, I come!*

Charlotte lived to the ripe age of eighty-two and, though for the most of her life weak and feeble in body, it was said that, "her spiritual horizon was for the most part cloudless". She kept an alert mind and a pen that was ever busy for her Master and composed about one hundred and fifty hymns and many poems besides. For the last two years of her life she was virtually bed-ridden and on September 22nd, 1871, she slipped away peacefully into the experience of what she had alluded to in her hymn of nearly forty years before.

> *Just as I am—of that free love*
>   *The breadth, length, depth and height to prove,*
> *Here for a season, then above—*
>   *O Lamb of God, I come!*

The words of this inspired hymn were, from the time of their writing, to be blessed to very many souls. In her lifetime Charlotte collected in a box one thousand letters from others, telling of spiritual help received through the words of her hymn. Indeed, her own brother, Henry Venn Elliott, fittingly testified of its usefulness, "In the course of a long ministry, I hope I have been permitted to see some fruit of my labours; but I feel far more has been done by a simple hymn of my sister's".

In St. Oswald's old churchyard at Grasmere in Westmoreland, there stand in a row the tombstones of the Wordsworth family. That of the poet's daughter, his "one and matchless daughter", Dora, bears the carving of a lamb—a lamb with a cross behind it. Someone had sent a copy of Charlotte's hymn to Dora as she lay seriously ill. The words of that hymn brought comfort and peace to her in her dying moments. "Why", she exclaimed when she first heard them, "that is the very thing for me", and asked for them oft-times as the end approached. When she died and her body was laid to rest in St. Oswald's churchyard, the tombstone with the carving of the lamb and the cross was erected and marks the spot today. On the bottom of the tombstone is inscribed a lovely Scripture text, "Him that cometh to me I will in no wise cast out" (John 6:37), the very same text that Charlotte Elliott put at the top of the page when she first penned her hymn.

In Bunyan's *Pilgrim's Progress*, Pilgrim saw similar words inscribed over the portal of the Pilgrim Gate, "Notwithstanding all that they have done before they come hither, they are in no wise cast out", and through that open Gate, with the assuring promise overhead, Pilgrim stepped onto the way that leads to eternal life.

> *Just as I am—Thou wilt receive,*
> *Wilt welcome, pardon, cleanse, relieve,*
> *Because Thy promise I believe—*
> *O Lamb of God, I come!*

This promise of the Saviour is absolutely trustworthy, "Him that cometh to Me I will in no wise cast out". Charlotte Elliott found it so, and millions beside have, in simple faith, stepped out upon it; none yet have found it wanting.

"Thou art the Everlasting Word"

Josiah Conder (1789-1855)

Josiah Conder.

This hymn was written in the early 19th century by a Congregational layman whose name was Josiah Conder. He was the fourth son of Thomas Conder, engraver and bookseller, and was born at Falcon Street, Aldersgate, London, on September 17th, 1789. Both his parents were staunch Noncomformists and young Josiah grew up in the atmosphere of a God-fearing home. When only five years of age he lost the sight of his right eye following vaccination against smallpox, and his parents, fearing for a possible harmful effect on the other eye, sent Josiah to Hackney for medical care. While there, he received schooling. His attending physician acted as his instructor and soon discerned in his young student a potential for a promising literary career.

In early life, Josiah began to exercise his talent and by the age of ten he was contributing essays to the *Monthly Precentor*. For these he was awarded two silver medals. At the age of fifteen he joined his father in the family metropolitan book-store and thereafter followed a strenuous literary career to become famous, not only as an author but also as an editor and publisher. In his twenty-first year he produced, in conjunction with some other like-minded young friends, a volume of poems, *The Associate Minstrels*. At the age of twenty-five he accepted the editorship of the *Electric Review* and a little later that also of a weekly newspaper, *The Patriot*. Both these editorships he carried for over twenty years and , "during that period", his biographer says, "he was in close association with the best literary people of that day, and was occupied with the publication of many works of his own, both in poetry and prose, mostly on religious topics". Besides his exhausting literary labours, Conder was a lay preacher and gave himself much to this work. His was a busy life; nevertheless, it was full for God. In the sixty-seventh year of his life his labours ended and he passed away at St. John's Wood, London, on December 27th, 1855.

The writings of Josiah Conder are a rich heritage. Endowed as he was with an outstanding natural ability, he developed this to the full by a lifetime's close contact with many of the literary giants of his day. Added to this was a deep spirituality and so from his pen have come some of the finest works, combining both literary and spiritual worth. His works cover a period of over fifty years and are very wide ranging in their scope. His prose is very diverse in its subject matter as may be detected from such titles as, *A Life of Bunyan*, *Epistle to the Hebrews* (a translation) or *The Modern Traveller*. This latter was the product of seven years' work and was published in thirty volumes, truly an outstanding feat for one who had himself never travelled abroad.

As a hymn-writer, Josiah Conder has a place of honour and ranks among the best of the early 19th century. His hymns were written amid the changing experiences, toils and trials of a busy life. At the time of his death he had collected all his own hymns into one volume. This collection, though ready for the press, was revised and published posthumously by his son, E. R. Conder, M.A., and entitled, *Hymns of Praise, Prayer and Devout Meditation.* In its preface, his son says that his father's hymns were, "transcripts of personal experience and add to the proofs so often given that God tunes the heart by trial and sorrow, not only to patience but to praise". Of Conder's hymns, William Garrett Horder comments, "The popularity of Conder's hymns may be gathered from the fact that at the present time more of them are in common usage in Great Britain and America than those of any other writer of the Congregational Body, Watts and Doddridge alone excepted . . . His finest hymns are marked by much elevation of thought expressed in language combining both force and beauty. They generally excel in unity, and in some the gradual unfolding of the leading idea is masterly".

Conder's hymns are the product of a deeply spiritual mind, and scriptural accuracy is the hallmark throughout. Probably nowhere is this more evident than in his majestic hymn on the Person of the Lord Jesus, "Thou art the Everlasting Word". John Nelson Darby is reported to have said that he would rather have been the writer of this one hymn than to have been the one writer of all other hymns. While today Conder's hymns are confined almost entirely to Congregational collections, this of all his compositions has found a worthy place in many other present-day hymnals:

> *Thou art the Everlasting Word,*
> *The Father's only Son,*
> *God manifestly seen and heard,*
> *And heaven's belovèd One.*
>
> > *Worthy O Lamb of God art Thou!*
> > *That every knee to Thee should bow.*
>
> *In Thee, most perfectly expressed,*
> *The Father's glories shine,*
> *Of the full Deity possessed,*
> *Eternally divine!*
>
> *True image of the Infinite,*
> *Whose essence is concealed;*
> *Brightness of uncreated light,*
> *The heart of God revealed.*

But the high myst'ries of His name
An angel's grasp transcend;
The Father only (glorious claim!)
The Son can comprehend.

Yet loving Thee, on whom His love
Ineffable doth rest,
Thy members all, in Thee, above,
As one with Thee are blest.

Throughout the universe of bliss,
The centre Thou, and Sun,
Th' eternal theme of praise is this,
To heaven's belovèd One.

The Lord Jesus, in the fulness of His person, is known to God alone. There are relationships within Deity too sacred and too sublime for angels to apprehend or for human hearts to appreciate. The languages of earth are too fettered to convey such heavenly mysteries. And yet, in wondrous grace, God the Son has become manifest in flesh and men are invited to ponder the majesty and mystery of His Divine person. Rays of glory shine out in the beautiful titles which He wears—"the image of the invisible God" (Col. 1:15), "the Son of the Father" (2 John 3), "the Lamb of God" (John 1:29). In such God-given terms and with becoming reverence, Conder in these majestic stanzas, addresses **HIM** whose absolute Deity and eternal Sonship are beyond all question and whose intrinsic glories are beyond compare.

"For in Him dwelleth all the fulness of the Godhead bodily" (Col. 2:9).

"Abide with me"

Henry Francis Lyte (1793-1847)

Henry Francis Lyte.

In the year 1800 two young boys were sent by their father from the village of Ednam in the Scottish Borders to Portora Royal Boarding School in Enniskillen, County Fermanagh, Ireland. Henry Francis Lyte, the younger of the two boys, was only seven years of age when he arrived in Enniskillen; his brother was just one year older. Separated from their parents and material support not forthcoming for their upkeep at the school, Dr. Burrows, their headmaster, took an active interest in them and became their benefactor and foster-father. Little did Dr. Burrows know then that Henry Francis Lyte would become the author of the dearly-loved and immortal hymn, "Abide with me".

The dispatch of the two Lyte brothers to school in Enniskillen marked the break-up of their family home in Ednam. Their father, Thomas Lyte, went to Jersey, their mother with their little brother left for London. Henry Francis never saw his mother again but he sorely missed her and in one of his boyhood poems he wrote affectionately of her, "Light of my heart and guardian of my youth". Lyte spent nine years at Portora and then entered Trinity College, Dublin, where he proved a very distinguished literary student, carrying off the prize for the best English poem of the University Year on three successive occasions.

He graduated B.A. and B.D. in 1815 and in the same year was appointed curate of Taghmon in County Wexford. Conditions there, however, adversely affected his health, and after two years, a complete change was needed. Lyte then crossed to France where he found the climate to be more congenial. His health greatly improved and within a year he returned from France to the South of England. There he fulfilled three short ministries; at Marazion, Sway and Charleton, and then in 1823 was appointed to Lower Brixham on the South Devonshire coast. Lyte's Brixham ministry was his real life's work and continued for twenty-four years, right up until the time of his death.

In Brixham, Lyte at first encountered hardship and opposition. The people there were rugged ungodly fishermen, Lyte was refined and cultured. Nevertheless, he loved the Brixham people and dearly loved their children. Slowly the old prejudices were broken down; the fishermen flocked to his services; the children were sent to his Sunday-school and there the attendances grew to some seven hundred and fifty pupils each Lord's day. As a consequence, Lyte's years at Brixham wrought great changes in that ungodly Devonshire town.

Lyte, besides, was a man of literary talent and in Brixham this aspect of his work occupied much of his time. He set to metre over sixty of the Psalms and these he published in 1834 as *The Spirit of the Psalms* ("Praise, my soul, the king of heaven", widely used as a hymn today, is Lyte's paraphrase of Psalm 103). At Brixham, "he made hymns for his little ones, and hymns for his hardy fishermen, and hymns for sufferers like himself". Some of these are still in use, of which "Jesus, I my cross have taken" and "My rest is in heaven" are favourites with many. He also was a poet of no mean distinction, his verse characterized by "sadness, tenderness and beauty". Notwithstanding, all the while Lyte longed that there might be something from his pen that would remain when he had gone.

> *I want not vulgar fame,*
> *I seek not to survive in brass or stone.*
> *Might verse of mine inspire*
> *One virtuous aim, one high resolve impart;*
> *Light in one drooping soul a hallowed fire,*
> *Or bind one broken heart—*
>
> *And grant me, swanlike, my last breath to spend*
> *In song that may not die!*

These lines, from his poem, "Declining Days", reflect the inner heart of the man, indeed, his life-long prayer. He was somehow aware that his crowning work in verse had yet to be written.

Lyte wrote his immortal "Swan Song" just two months before he died. He was then fifty-four years of age. His health had for some years been slowly deteriorating and it was necessary for him to spend the winter months in a kinder Mediterranean climate. In a letter to a friend in early September 1847 he commented on the approaching winter, "I am meditating flight again to the South. The little faithful robin is every morning at my window, sweetly warning me that autumnal hours are at hand. The swallows are preparing for flight and inviting me to accompany them, and yet, alas! while I talk of flying, I am just able to crawl".

Lord's day, September 5th, 1847, was Lyte's last Sunday with his own dearly-loved people of Brixham, and though a sick man, he resolved to minister to them once more. Taking as his text 1 Cor. 11:26, he spoke to them his last message, and then retired to his home on Berry Head. Feeling exhausted, he rested in the afternoon and then in the evening went out to sit by the edge of the cliff. It was a lovely sunset over Torbay and Dartmoor; he felt that the sun of his own life was westering and going down. A glorious sunshine, however, flooded his soul; its rays were golden. His musings centred on the lovely text of Luke 24:29, "Abide with us:

for it is toward evening, and the day is far spent". The moment had come—it was "an inspiration, an answer to prayer, a divine illumination" and there flowed from Lyte's pen his immortal "Swan Song".

> *Abide with me! fast falls the eventide,*
> *The darkness thickens. Lord, with me abide,*
> *When other helpers fail, and comforts flee;*
> *Help of the helpless, O abide with me!*
>
> *Swift to its close ebbs out life's little day,*
> *Earth's joys grow dim, its glories pass away.*
> *Change and decay in all around I see*
> *O Thou who changest not, abide with me.*
>
> *Not a brief glance I beg, a passing word;*
> *But as Thou dwellest with Thy disciples Lord,*
> *Familiar, condescending, patient, free,*
> *Come not to sojourn, but abide with me.*
>
> *Come not in terrors, as the King of Kings,*
> *But kind and good, with healing in Thy wings,*
> *Tears for all woes, a heart for every plea,*
> *Come, Friend of Sinners, and abide with me.*
>
> *Thou on my head in early youth did smile,*
> *And though rebellious and perverse meanwhile,*
> *Thou has not left me, oft as I left Thee*
> *On to the close, O Lord, abide with me!*
>
> *I need Thy presence every passing hour;*
> *What but Thy grace can foil the tempter's power?*
> *Who like Thyself my guide and stay can be?*
> *Through cloud and sunshine, O abide with me.*
>
> *I fear no foe with Thee at hand to bless;*
> *Ills have no weight and tears no bitterness:*
> *Where is death's sting? Where, grave, thy victory?*
> *I triumph still, if Thou abide with me.*

Hold Thou Thy cross before my closing eyes;
Speak through the gloom, and point me to the skies:
Heaven's morning breaks, and earth's vain shadows flee!
In life, in death, O Lord, abide with me!

Lyte left the same week for the South of France, where he died at Nice two months later. The end came on November 20th, 1847. It was glorious. As he stood on the threshold of life's exit doorway, his heart yearned for companionship, one who could go with him all the way. The Christ who had been through death and had been his personal companion through life, would not fail him now. Of that he was confident and exclaimed, "Oh, there is nothing terrible in death, Jesus Christ steps down into the grave before me" and, pointing his finger to the sky and heavenward, he breathed out his last words, "peace . . . joy".

Lyte's hymn, "Abide with me", was sung for the first time at his memorial service in his beloved Brixham and since then, at eight o'clock each evening, the bells of the Parish Church peel out its notes to the fishermen as they put out to sea. Lyte, when he wrote the words, composed for them an accompanying tune but the popular tune "Eventide" to which the hymn has become so gracefully wedded was composed fourteen years later by Dr. W. H. Monk. Dr. Monk, at that time, had just passed through a time of deep sorrow, having lost his first child, a little three year old daughter. One evening as he and his wife, with sorrowing hearts, stood and watched a lovely sunset, the lines of Lyte's hymn flooded his mind. "Heaven's morning breaks and earth's vain shadows flee". The music then flowed spontaneously and he wrote it down. In all it took about ten minutes and Monk felt that it had been Divinely given.

This hymn is immortal. Its singing has marked many historic occasions throughout the past century and has been a favourite with kings, queens and presidents. It has been sung over and over again at Wembley. It was sung on the beaches of Dunkirk and in the cloisters of Westminster Abbey. It was sung at Khartoum, as General Gordon waited patiently and with apprehension, and in the Antarctic as Sir Ernest Shackleton lay on his deathbed. Nurse Edith Cavell, as she went to execution in Brussels, was attended by Mr. Gahan, the British Consul; together they repeated very softly and very slowly the words of "Abide with me"; when the moment of parting came she clasped his hand with a smile, "We shall meet again—heaven's morning breaks and earth's vain shadows flee", and turning away she was heard to quietly breathe, "In life, in death, O Lord, abide with me".

"This hymn", says Dr. Boreham, "assures us that, so long as the world stands, no man need be lonely who will extend the hospitalities of his soul to One who loves to abide with all who will court His company". It was so at the doorway at Emmaus on the resurrection evening when Cleopas and his companion constrained the risen Saviour to come in and abide. It was so for Henry Francis Lyte at the age of twenty-five when, as a needy and lonely sinner, he admitted the same Saviour, threw wide open the door of his heart and life to Him who had pledged to be an unfailing companion along life's highway, and through that valley where the darkness deepens and other helpers fail and comforts flee. Never did his Saviour at any time ever fail that pledge.

"Sweet feast of love divine!"

Edward Denny (1796-1889)

Sir Edward Denny.

"It is especially pleasing for the Christian to enumerate among the 'poets of the sanctuary' and sweet singers of the Master, one whose advantages of birth, fortune and title raise him above the level of his fellow-believers". Such a lofty appraisal by Hy. Pickering, of the one who is the subject of this present study, awakes our immediate interest.

Edward Denny, the eldest son of Sir Edward and Lady Elizabeth Denny of Tralee Castle, Co. Kerry, Ireland, was born on October

2nd, 1796, at No. 1 Merrion Square, Dublin, the town residence of his maternal grandfather, Judge Robert Day, M.P. Edward was educated at Eton and at Exeter College, Oxford. At twenty-two he was M.P. for Tralee; at thirty-one he was High Sheriff of Kerry; at thirty-five he succeeded his father as fourth Baronet, as Lord of the Manors of Dennyvale and Castlemore (the estates amounting to some twenty-nine thousand acres, including practically the whole of the town of Tralee with a rent roll of about twenty-five thousand pounds a year). It seemed likely that this world would have early engulfed in its stream such a one, born of this high degree with its many advantages of wealth and honour but, in a most remarkable way, Edward was drawn from its fast-flowing current by an Almighty Hand. As a young man, he was brought under conviction of sin and his need of salvation through the reading of a book (*Father Clement*) and ever afterwards testified that it was to that book that he owed his conversion to God.

Conversion's experience radically changed Edward's lifestyle. He publicly confessed His Saviour and early identified himself with the people of God, meeting after a simple New Testament pattern. The greater part of his life was lived in London and there he was closely linked with the Park Walk assembly. In that assembly and throughout the London area, for many years and in a quiet and unassuming way, Sir Edward ministered to the saints of God. Among them he was a brother beloved, highly esteemed and greatly appreciated. His devoted service for God continued right into his ninety-third year and he passed away peacefully at his London residence, "The Grove", Boltons, South Kensington, on June 13th, 1889.

Sir Edward's love for his Lord found expression in sacrificial ministry. In material things, he was ever kind and generous to others while at the same time, so far as he personally was concerned, a little money went a long way. In spiritual things, he ministered bountifully to the saints. His store was rich and ever full and from it he drew liberally for the flock of God. His bright personal intellect, his higher education and a deep insight into the truths of the Word of God all served to lend weight and character to his oral and written ministries.

His writings were, in the main, on prophetic subjects. One of his earliest and most comprehensive was entitled A *Prophetic Stream of Time* in which he outlined God's dealings with man from the creation to the end of all things. Many of his writings were illustrated by chart or diagram which served to elucidate the particular subject under consideration.

As a hymn-writer, Sir Edward ranks among the best. Indeed, his hymns and poems are his most outstanding literary legacy. Some of his earliest compositions were compiled as A *Selection of Hymns* (1839). In 1848, the first edition of his *Hymns and Poems* was published and further editions were released in the years that followed. This work of verse, rich in both its literary and spiritual qualities, contains such precious and endearing hymns as,

> "A pilgrim through this lonely world"
> "Bride of the Lamb, awake! awake!"
> "Bright with all His crowns of glory"
> "Light of the lonely pilgrim's heart"
> "Oh! what a lonely path were ours"
> "O wondrous hour! when, Jesus, Thou"
> "Sweet feast of love divine!"
> " 'Tis finish'd all—our souls to win"
> " 'Tis past, the dark and dreary night!"
> "To Calvary, Lord, in spirit now"
> "What grace, O Lord, and beauty shone!"
> "While in sweet communion feeding".

The hymns of Sir Edward Denny were the product of his heart's musings upon great Scriptural truths. The return of the Lord Jesus was the theme of many of his compositions, and these, his "Millennial Hymns", reveal his deep insight into the dispensational teaching of Scripture; in them the respective roles, realms and blessings of the Church, the nation of Israel and the Gentile nations are clearly preserved throughout. The pilgrim character of the believer was another favourite theme, and in these hymns Denny exhorts the saints to pattern their lifestyle after the example of the "Heavenly Stranger".

> *The cords that bound my heart to earth*
> *Were broken by His hand;*
> *Before His cross I found myself*
> *A stranger in the land.*

The theme of love was, however, the grandest and sweetest of all his subjects. Denny's estimate of love was great, sourced in the heart of God and eternal in its sweep. In his hymns, he portrays love as motivating and marking every movement and ministry of the Saviour, and love as providing for the saints in this dispensation a precious weekly feast:

Sweet feast of love divine!
'Tis grace that makes us free
To feed upon this bread and wine,
In memory, Lord, of Thee.

Here every welcome guest
Waits, Lord, from Thee to learn
The secrets of Thy Father's breast,
And all Thy grace discern.

Here conscience ends its strife,
And faith delights to prove
The sweetness of the bread of life,
The fulness of Thy love.

That blood that flow'd for sin
In symbol here we see,
And feel the blessèd pledge within,
That we are loved of Thee.

Oh! if this glimpse of love
Is so divinely sweet,
What will it be, O Lord, above,
Thy gladdening smile to meet!

To see Thee face to face,
Thy perfect likeness wear,
And all Thy ways of wondrous grace
Through endless years declare.

This precious weekly feast for the saints is the Lord's supper. Divine love spreads the table; Divine grace issues the invitation and bestows the fitness to be there. The symbols upon the table are the bread and the cup, divinely chosen and unmistakable. The saints partake of them and remember their Lord. Such remembrance of Him is "divinely sweet"; nevertheless, it is at best but a glimpse, a foretaste of a glorious future gathering, when like and with their Saviour they will not need symbols any more.

"And is it so? I shall be like Thy Son!"

John Nelson Darby (1800-1882)

John Nelson Darby.

Leap Castle lies today in ruins, its burnt-out ivy-covered shell now a haven for the wild birds. Nevertheless, its commanding situation together with its impressive keep tower overlooking the valley to the Slieve Bloom mountains tell of a past glory. It was originally built in the 14th century as a fortification to guard the pass into Munster and was at one time the home of the Darby family in King's county (Offaly), Ireland. But why did John Nelson Darby, as a young man of no meagre intellect and

131

education turn his back on such splendour and wealth? What was it that induced him to leave it all to become virtually a homeless traveller? The answer to this quest is to be found in some lines written by himself in his middle years of life,

'Tis the treasure I've found in His love
That has made me a pilgrim below.

He had weighed things wisely and concluded with Paul that "the things which are seen are temporal; but the things which are not seen are eternal." (2 Cor. 4:18). He had found other treasure—satisfying treasure, treasure out-wearing the years of time and undiminishing in eternity.

John Nelson Darby, the youngest son of John Darby, a well-to-do land owner and merchant of Markley, Sussex, England and of Leap Castle, Ireland was born at his father's London house in Westminster on November 18th, 1800. His middle name "Nelson" was received from his god-father, the great Lord Nelson, under whom an uncle, Admiral, Sir Henry Darby, K.C.B., had served at the Battle of the Nile. Darby's mother died when he was only a boy.

Darby received his early education at Westminster School and at the age of fifteen entered Trinity College, Dublin, where he graduated as Classical Gold Medallist at the age of nineteen. In due course, he entered the legal profession and was called to the Irish Chancery Bar. A promising professional career stretched out before him and many had high hopes that he would rise to its highest honours. But God was calling him, and so after deep spiritual exercise he abandoned his legal profession and stepped out on a life of spiritual service. First he entered the Established Church and was ordained deacon in 1825, serving for a time as curate of the large and straggling parish of Calary in Co. Wicklow. In this, he gave himself unreservedly to the work, ministering physically and spiritually to the needs of the poor of that desolate bog-land parish.

Darby soon discerned an unparalleled apathy within the Established Church where very few cared for the souls of men. He looked at the Dissenting churches around him and detected in them a cold exclusiveness which he felt to be contrary to the spirit of Christ. Thus bewildered, he turned to God and to His Word for he felt that there he should find clear guidance as to his path in life. He soon became convinced that his position within the Established Church was no longer tenable and he resigned from his parochial charge. At that same time others in and around the city of Dublin were likewise searching the Scriptures, and the Spirit of God opened up to their hearts the great truth, as expressed later by Henry Groves, of, "the oneness of the church of God, involving a fellowship large enough to embrace all saints and narrow enough to exclude the world". Prayerfully, they followed the path that God had revealed through His Word and in the latter part of the 1820's, Darby with some others gathered for the first time to observe the Lord's Supper. A room in Fitzwilliam Square in the city of Dublin was their place of meeting but the Lord Himself was their gathering centre, the Word of God was their guide, and the Spirit of God presided in their gatherings. Those were precious days.

Darby, though he had resigned the curacy, had not resigned the ministry of God's Word. He regarded the whole world as his parish and travelled widely throughout Great Britain, Ireland, France, Germany, Switzerland, Holland, Italy, Canada, America and Australia carrying the gospel and teaching the Church of God great New Testament truths. The secret of his ministry was a deep devotion to Christ Jesus his Lord and under his ministry, thousands separated themselves from the Established Church and gathered simply to the Name of the Lord Jesus.

Darby's manner of life was marked by simplicity, sincerity and severity. Recognizing that this world could not be mended, he lived apart from its ways and was known to say, "the world goes its own way and I am not of it". He had not respect of persons and loved all who were spiritually minded and devoted to Christ, irrespective of their rank or name. He was generous to those in need, sympathetic to the afflicted, patient with the ignorant and kind to all. For the cause of Christ, he sacrificed much and in life bore many afflictions and heartbreaks. In these he committed his cause to God and though misunderstood by many on earth, he was happy in knowing that he was understood in Heaven.

John Nelson Darby served his Lord throughout life faithfully and devotedly—a powerful personality, a spiritual giant, a mystic engrossed in the heavenlies. On April, 29th, 1882, he fell asleep in Christ and was laid to rest in Wimborne Road Cemetery,

Bournemouth, where the spot is marked by a simple tombstone bearing his epitaph,

JOHN NELSON DARBY
"AS UNKNOWN AND WELL KNOWN"
DEPARTED TO BE WITH CHRIST,
29th APRIL, 1882.
AGE 81
II COR. V:21

Lord let me wait for Thee alone,
My life be only this—
To serve Thee here on earth unknown,
Then share Thy Heavenly bliss.
J.N.D.

John Nelson Darby (J.N.D.) is probably best known for his writings, and for his translations of Holy Scripture. His *New Translation* of the Bible from the original languages into English bears the marks of true scholarship and spirituality. He also translated the Bible into French and German. His *Synopsis of the Books of the Bible* is a masterly summary of the teachings of both Old and New Testaments. The varied writings of J.N.D. are gathered together in more than forty volumes of *Collected Writings, Notes and Comments, Notes and Jottings* and several volumes of *Letters,* and represent a written ministry during more than fifty years of busy service. His tracts and pamphlets are far-seeing, almost prophetic in character, as, for example, his *Progress of Democratic Power and its effect on the Moral State of England.*

Darby, however, was also a prolific hymn-writer and a volume of *Spiritual Songs* has preserved his hymns to us as a rich legacy. J.N.D.'s hymns, like his writings, are scholarly and spiritual, born out of deep devotion to Christ. Beautiful verse gives expression to great spiritual truths. For personal meditation and adoration, or for collective worship, here is a rare treasure indeed. Of his hymns in common usage today, the following are, perhaps, the best known:

> "And is it so? I shall be like Thy Son!"
> "Hark! ten thousand voices crying"
> "I'm waiting for Thee, Lord"

"Rest of the saints above"
"Rise, my soul! Thy God directs thee"
"This world is a wilderness wide"

His hymn, "And is it so? I shall be like Thy Son!" is one of the best loved that have come from his pen. It was written in 1872 and entitled, "The Hope of Day".

And is it so? I shall be like Thy Son!
  Is this the grace which He for me has won?
Father of glory! Thought beyond all thought;
  In glory to His Own blest likeness brought.

O Jesus, Lord; who loved me like to Thee?
  Fruit of Thy work! With Thee too, there to see
Thy glory, Lord, while endless ages roll,—
  Myself the prize and travail of Thy soul.

Yet it must be! Thy love had not its rest,
  Were Thy redeemed not with Thee fully blest;
That love that gives not as the world, but shares
  All it possesses, with its loved co-heirs!

Nor I alone; Thy loved ones all, complete,
  In glory round Thee there with joy shall meet!
All like Thee; for Thy glory like Thee, Lord!
  Object supreme of all, by all adored!

The heart is satisfied; can ask no more;
  All thought of self is now for ever o'er;
Christ, its unmingled Object, fills the heart
  In blest adoring love—its endless part.

Darby here transports our spirits to an eternal day—a day when aspiration and anticipation give way to realization—a day when self with all its ugliness recedes, and for ever we be like God's Son. Then every heart will know its perfect rest—the heart of the Son as satisfied with the fruit of His soul's dark travail, the heart of the saint as resplendent in the likeness of his Saviour, and the heart of the Father as beholding each one reflecting perfectly the image of His beloved Son.

"With Jesus in our midst"

Robert Cleaver Chapman (1803-1902)

Robert Cleaver Chapman.

Towards the close of the last century, a letter posted in a foreign country and addressed, "R. C. Chapman, University of Love, England" was duly delivered to its correct destination in a narrow cul-de-sac among the slums of Barnstaple in County Devon. There the home of this great "apostle of love" was located at No. 6 New Buildings. Though that little terrace house seemed unpretentious and its furnishings meagre and simple, its atmosphere was the very air of heaven. A visitor who had once spent some time there as guest of that spiritual giant, subsequently bore eloquent testimony to his host: "I learned that he was pre-eminently holy, a man who rose early, and prayed much, and always walked with God", and on the occasion of Mr. Chapman's ninety-ninth birthday a press reporter paid tribute to him: "No one can estimate the influence that has been created by the saintly life and beautiful faith and glorious example of Robert Chapman".

But who was this remarkable Robert C. Chapman?

Robert Cleaver Chapman was born into a family of nobility and wealth at Elsinore, Denmark in 1803. His father, Thomas Chapman, a well-to-do merchant had earlier come from Whitby in Yorkshire, England. Robert enjoyed a childhood of luxury. He received early private education under a Roman Catholic French Abbè and later schooling in Yorkshire; at the age of fifteen he went to London to study Law. After five years of arduous study, he was admitted an Attorney of the Court of Common Pleas and an Attorney of the Court of Kings Bench. Professional opportunities opened out before him; the social round of London's West End made its appeal; Robert Chapman was then only twenty years of age.

Robert C. Chapman was a young man of high moral standards, blameless in character and one who sought to obtain the salvation of God by his own self-righteousness. One night, however, while sitting under the ministry of James Harrington Evans in John Street Chapel, he appreciated that his garment of self-righteousness was in reality before God only a filthy rag. He discarded it and embraced the Lord Jesus as his personal Saviour. Writing later of that event he said, "In the good and set time Thou spakest to me saying, 'This is the rest wherewith ye may cause the weary to rest; and this is the refreshing' (Isaiah 28:12). And how sweet Thy words, 'Son, be of good cheer, thy sins be forgiven thee' (Matthew 9:2). How precious the sight of the Lamb of God! And how glorious the robe of righteousness hiding from the holy eyes of my Judge all my sin and pollution."

From the moment of conversion, Chapman sought to be true to his Saviour and Lord. Confessing Christ proved costly both in his own family circle and among his professional colleagues. He sought to obey his Lord in baptism and approached James Harrington Evans on the matter. "You will wait a while, and consider the matter" advised the pastor. "No, I will make haste and delay not to keep His commandments" replied Chapman and was forthwith baptised. He devoted himself to the service of Christ and to the service of others, working among the poor and needy of the slums of London. Besides a big heart for needy souls, Chapman had a tender conscience and desired to be well-pleasing to his Lord. After deep exercise of heart and prayerful consideration, he relinquished his profession, gave away his personal fortune, dedicated himself to full-time service for Christ and at the age of twenty-nine left London for Barnstaple in the West Country, there to become pastor of Ebenezer Street Baptist Chapel, accepting the charge on one condition, "That I should be free to teach **all** I found written in the Scriptures".

God showed to such an open, honest and enquiring heart precious truths from His Word, and Chapman longed that these be made known among the saints—that the unity of God's children was not dependent on any rite or ceremony, that ministry was a matter of Divine gift and not of human or ecclesiastical ordination, that priestly service was the spiritual birthright of all believers and when the Lord's supper was observed in simplicity that there should be liberty for all brethren to take part as led by the Spirit of God. These truths Chapman proclaimed in love and waited patiently and prayerfully for the Spirit of God to write them upon the hearts of the saints.

Chapman was noted for his grace and yieldingness, but always dealt in firmness and faithfulness to his Lord when there was error, while at the same time always showing kindness to the erring ones. Such loving conduct was God-glorifying and was Chapman's strength. He was truly "a brother beloved". In all matters, he exhibited the spirit of his Lord and honoured the injunction of Phil. 2:3, "Let nothing be done through strife or vainglory; but in lowliness of mind let each esteem other better than themselves" and was often heard to say, "Humility is the secret of fellowship and pride the secret of division". His ministry among the saints was a ministry of love and of reconciliation. To a brother with whom he differed in certain things, he wrote, "We judged it a cause for self-humiliation that we could not fully agree, but not a reason for strife and separation. God would soon make all His children one, did they always set their faces like the cherubim towards the mercy-seat".

Chapman's ministry among the unconverted in Barnstaple was

also greatly blessed of God. The people there listened to the "man of God" whom they knew and who lived Christ daily in their midst, and as a result many souls were saved in that Devonshire town which, at that time, was marked by misery and drunkenness. He loved to preach in the open air and in cottage meetings. His own home was open always and there many a needy soul found help and blessing; in that simple dwelling the Lord's people were always welcome to stay as long as they pleased and never once in seventy years were any turned away.

Chapman's life was truly remarkable and yet there was nothing ostentatious about it. Though a gifted minister of the Word of God, he would never consent to the publication of his ministry. When friends asked him, "Why don't you write your life story?", he replied, "It is written already and will be published in the Morning". In the same spirit, R. C. Chapman composed hymns for the benefit and the blessing of the people of God. Most were written during his early years at Barnstaple and some one hundred and sixty-five have been preserved for us. His simple hymn, "With Jesus in our midst", is familiar to saints meeting in assembly fellowship and is a great favourite with many:

> With Jesus in our midst,
>   We gather round the board;
> Though many, we are one in Christ,
>   One body in the Lord.
>
> Our sins were laid on Him
>   When bruised on Calvary;
> With Christ we died and rose again,
>   And sit with Him on high.
>
> Faith eats the bread of life,
>   And drinks the living wine;
> Thus we, in love together knit,
>   On Jesus' breast recline.
>
> Soon shall the night be gone,
>   And we with Jesus reign;
> The marriage supper of the Lamb
>   Shall banish all our pain.

This short hymn expresses in simple words a tremendous twofold truth—that the saints of God are intimately and indissolubly linked with their Lord and that the saints of God are intimately and indissolubly linked with one another. These twin truths, so very precious to the heart of R. C. Chapman, are beautifully epitomized in his hymn. The hymn befits the Lord's supper, the occasion above all others when these truths are so perfectly expressed—that, through grace, we have become one with Christ and one with every saint of God.

"O Lord of heaven and earth and sea"

Christopher Wordsworth (1807-1885)

Christopher Wordsworth.

The congregation of the little country parish church at Standford-in-the-Vale cum Goosey in Berkshire, England, had been very niggardly in their giving and week by week the collection remained meagre. At length and with exercise of heart, their minister, Christopher Wordsworth spoke to them of the duty and privilege of giving and finally decided to write for them a hymn. The hymn, consisting originally of nine stanzas, was sung

141

repeatedly in that little Berkshire church and besides achieving a very practical outcome, has come down to us in all its richness and beauty.

O Lord of heaven, and earth, and sea
To Thee all praise and glory be;
How shall we show our love to Thee,
     Giver of all?

The golden sunshine, vernal air,
Sweet flowers and fruits, Thy love declare;
Where harvests ripen, Thou art there,
     Giver of all.

Thou didst not spare Thine only Son,
But gav'st Him for a world undone;
And freely with that blessèd One
     Thou givest all.

We lose what on ourselves we spend,
We have as treasure without end
Whatever, Lord, to Thee we lend,
     Who givest all.

Whatever, Lord, we lend to Thee
Repaid a thousandfold will be;
Then gladly will we give to Thee,
     Giver of all.

Christopher Wordsworth was the nephew of the famous poet-laureate, William Wordsworth, and the son of Christopher and Priscilla Wordsworth. He was born on October 30th, 1807 at Lambeth, the youngest of three brothers, all of whom in later years gained high distinction as prize men at their universities. Christopher's education was first at Winchester and later at Trinity College, Cambridge. He matriculated at Trinity College in 1826 and following a brilliant career there, in which he carried off an unprecedented number of university and college prizes, graduated with many honours in 1830. On graduation he was elected a Fellow of the College and engaged as Classical Lecturer, and in 1836 was chosen as Public Orator for the university. During his Trinity days, he travelled widely in Greece and the record of his travels he published in his *Athens and Attica* (1836).

In 1836, Wordsworth was elected Headmaster of Harrow School, an outstanding distinction for someone still under thirty years of age. In 1844, he was appointed by Sir Robert Peel as Canon of Westminster and six years later, he accepted the living of Standford-in-the-Vale cum Goosey where for nineteen years he ministered faithfully as vicar in that quiet parish in Berkshire. In 1869, he was elected Bishop of Lincoln, a post which he held for fifteen years, resigning just a few months before his death on March 21st, 1885.

Christopher Wordsworth has been described as, "a fine scholar, a great and good man". He was renowned as the most celebrated Greek scholar of his day, and with an enormous working capacity he became a prolific writer. In 1851, he published his *Memoirs of William Wordsworth*, a fitting record of the great poet of Rydal Mount with whom he had kept in close touch over the years by visitation and by pen right up till his uncle's death in 1850. His monumental work *A Commentary on the whole Bible*, which might have been a long life's labour for any scholar, was completed in the years 1856-1870, and in this notable commentary Wordsworth makes Scripture interpret Scripture. Other publications appeared with regularity and included, besides books, volumes of sermons, tracts, pamphlets, letters, addresses and speeches.

As a hymn-writer, Christopher Wordsworth contributed with distinction. He regarded, "the first duty of a hymn-writer to teach sound doctrine". The subject matter of his verse was varied and he wrote hymns for almost every season of the church's year. These he compiled and published in 1862 as *The Holy Year* which was in essence a calendar of hymns containing one hundred and seventeen of his own compositions and eighty-two hymns from other sources. Francis Arthur Jones says of Wordsworth that he "wrote his hymns at all sorts of odd moments and in all sorts of places—in the train, riding or during a walk. If at night he was unable to sleep, he would get up and compose a few verses. The hymns were written on the backs of envelopes, small scraps of sermon paper or even on the margin of the book he happened to be reading. He was an extremely rapid writer but spared no pains in correcting till the composition satisfied him".

Of Wordsworth, as a hymn-writer and as a man, John Ellerton has this to say, "Christopher Wordsworth, Bishop of Lincoln, is one of whom we certainly do not just think as a writer of hymns but as a great scholar, a diligent and careful expositor, an accurate theologian and controversialist, a great and wise ruler in the church and a most holy, humble, loving, self-denying man. And the man is reflected in his verse. To read one of his best hymns is to look into a plain face, without one striking feature, but with an irresistible charm of honesty, intelligence and affection."

Great hymns full of great truth have come from Wordsworth's pen, and include:

"See the Conqueror mounts in triumph", telling of the glorious ascension of the Lord Jesus,

"Gracious Spirit, Holy Ghost", paraphrasing the apostle Paul's great chapter on love (I Cor. 13),

"The Galilean Fishers toil", portraying the Lord Jesus, coming, as of old, in the dark experiences of life,

"O day of rest and gladness", speaking of the blessedness and beauty of the Lord's day,

"Hark! the sound of holy voices", picturing the redeemed of the ages, beyond tribulation, and engaged in triumphant song.

"O Lord of heaven and earth and sea" is Wordsworth's best known hymn. In it, he speaks of the greatness and of the goodness of God. All creation, daily and in every land, are the recipients of His beneficence. Egerton Young, who opened up the Nelson river district with the gospel was one day surrounded by three hundred wild Indians. He read aloud to them and for some four hours expounded the sublime truth of John 3:16, "God so loved the world that He gave His only begotten Son". Their hearts were touched. They had never heard it before. When he had finished the principal chief stepped forward and spoke, "Missionary", he said, "God...I see His goodness in giving us the moose, the reindeer, the beaver and the bear. I see His loving-kindness in sending us, when the south winds blow, the ducks and geese; and when the snow and ice melt away, and our lakes and rivers are open again, I see how He fills them with fish. I have watched all this for years, and I have felt that the Great Spirit, so kind and watchful and loving...but what you have just said fills my heart and satisfies my longing..."

Truly God is the "Giver of All"; of this there can be no dispute for He has given His Son, and "how shall He not with Him also freely give us all things?" (Rom. 8:32)

Such beneficence can never be fully repaid. Nevertheless, our hearts have been touched by its bounty and would like to give something in return. Whatever we give, however, is merely a sending back of what God has already given to us. David, at the close of life, after he had poured out all his treasure unto the Lord freely admitted, "For all things come of Thee, and of Thine own have we given Thee" (1 Chr. 29:14), "O LORD our God, all this store...cometh of Thine hand and is all Thine own" (1 Chr. 29:16).

Nor is God only the Great Giver; He will yet be the Great Recompenser.

> *Whatever, Lord, we lend to Thee*
> *Repaid a thousandfold will be;*
> *Then gladly will we give to Thee,*
> *Giver of all.*

"Lamb of God! our souls adore Thee"

James George Deck (1807-1884)

James George Deck.

James George Deck was born of a godly Huguenot family at Bury St. Edmunds on November 1st, 1807. His father, John Deck was the postmaster there. His mother was a godly woman whose burden in life was the spiritual welfare of her family. She believed in prayer and adopted the practice of regularly setting aside time each day to be alone with God and pray for the family. Her prayers were answered and she had the unspeakable joy of seeing all her family of eight children led to Christ and consecrating their lives to

His service. One of her daughters, Mary Jane (Mary Jane Walker) became the authoress of several well-known and good hymns as, "I journey through a desert drear and wild", "Jesus I will trust Thee, trust Thee with my soul", "O spotless Lamb of God, in Thee" and "The wanderer no more will roam".

James George Deck, as a young man, studied in Paris under one of Napoleon's generals and at the age of seventeen went to India as an officer in army service. While there, God spoke to him in a very definite way, teaching him the sinfulness and need of his own heart. He resolved to do better, and drew up a code of good resolutions, signing it with his own blood. He soon found, however, that he had not the strength to keep it, such was the weakness of the flesh. In 1826, Deck returned to England after a severe attack of cholera and later in the same year, through the instrumentality of his sister Clara, came under the ministry of a godly Anglican clergyman and was brought to Christ for salvation. He was then nineteen years of age.

In 1829, Deck married Alicia Field, daughter of Samuel Field, an evangelical clergyman and in the following year returned to India. There he boldly witnessed for Christ among his colleagues with the result that a number were brought to a saving faith in Christ. In 1835, Deck returned again to England having, for conscience sake, resigned his commission. His exercise then was to enter the Church of England as a minister but while staying at the home of his father-in-law in County Devon, an incident happened which changed the whole course of his life. The occasion was the christening of his second son. There were some present who questioned the scriptural authority for such a practice and this caused Deck deep exercise of heart. He searched the Scriptures but nowhere could he find any basis for "baptismal regeneration". Nevertheless, it was contained in the *Book of Common Prayer of the Church of England*. What was he to do? Having left the army to enter the Church of England, he now saw that the teaching of this church was not supported by the Word of God. In his dilemma he referred the problem to his wife and her clear reply, "Whatever you believe to be the will of God, do it at any cost" gave him guidance as to his path. Deck continued to search his New Testament and very shortly afterwards joined the fellowship of other like-minded believers gathered to the precious Name of the Lord Jesus.

Deck began to witness for Christ and preach the gospel throughout the county of Devon. Many believed, and he taught them from the Word of God the truths of believers' baptism and regularly gathering to remember the Lord while awaiting His return from Heaven. After some fourteen years of active service for the Lord around the towns and villages of the West country, Deck suffered a breakdown in health. A complete change was recommended by his medical advisers and in 1852, James George Deck, his wife and family of eight children sailed for New Zealand.

The Decks arrived in Wellington, New Zealand, aboard the ship *Cornwall* in the latter part of 1852. They purchased land and as a family settled in Waiwera near to Motueka in the Nelson province of the South Island. Shortly after their arrival, Deck's beloved wife Alicia died and was laid to rest in Motueka cemetery. Deck remarried in 1855; five more children were born, but shortly after the birth of the fifth baby (Martin Luther) his second wife and her new-born baby both died from a severe attack of measles. Though times were difficult, Deck's faith in God stood firm. He faithfully witnessed for Christ in this new land of his adoption, at first in the Motueka district and then more widely throughout New Zealand.

For over thirty years James George Deck preached the gospel and taught the Word of God in New Zealand. Though there were many difficulties there was much fruit and little assemblies were raised up to the Lord's Name. Shortly after their second bereavement the Decks, as a family, moved to the city of Wellington in the North Island and lived there for several years but in the early 1870's, Mr. Deck's health started to fail and he returned to Motueka. There he died on August 14th, 1884, and three days later, his body was laid to rest in the Motueka cemetery on the foreshore.

Deck's influence for God as an evangelist and Bible teacher remains still in evidence in the West country of England and even more so throughout New Zealand. Nevertheless, it is as hymn-writer and poet that he is best remembered. His compositions extended over a period of many years though most of his best hymns were written in the years 1838-1844 when, as a young man in his thirties, he preached the gospel around Devon and Somerset. Some one hundred and one of his hymns and sixty-five of his poems were collected together in his *Hymns and Sacred Poems* and published in 1876. In its preface Deck says, "I have sought rather to render the Hymns scriptural and true in their tone and character, than to please the natural ear and taste, by an attempt at poetic composition".

Deck's hymns were written mostly for believers and breathe a deep spirit of worship. Many of them are particularly suited for use at the Lord's supper and include such favourites as:

> "'A little while', our Lord shall come"
> "'Abba, Father'!, we approach Thee"
> "Lamb of God! our souls adore Thee"
> "Lamb of God! Thou now art seated"
> "Lord Jesus, are we one with Thee?"
> "Lord, we would ne'er forget thy love"
> "O Jesus Lord! 'tis joy to know"
> "O Lamb of God, still keep me"
> "O Lord, when we the path retrace"
> "The veil is rent. Lo! Jesus stands"
> "We bless our Saviour's name"

The hymns, "Lamb of God! our souls adore Thee" and "Lamb of God! Thou now art seated" were written by Deck in 1838. They originally appeared as two parts of one hymn and were entitled, "The Lamb of God". Each part had four verses.

Part I

Lamb of God! our souls adore Thee,
*   While upon Thy face we gaze;*
There the Father's love and glory
*   Shine in all their brightest rays:*
Thy almighty power and wisdom
*   All creation's works proclaim;*
Heaven and earth alike confess Thee
*   As the ever great "I AM".*

Son of God! Thy Father's bosom
*   Ever was Thy dwelling-place;*
His delight, in Him rejoicing,
*   One with Him in power and grace:*
Oh, what wondrous love and mercy!
*   Thou didst lay Thy glory by,*
And for us didst come from heaven,
*   As the Lamb of God, to die.*

Lamb of God! when we behold Thee
Lowly in the manger laid;
Wand'ring as a homeless Stranger,
In the world Thy hands had made;
When we see Thee in the garden,
In Thine agony of blood;
At Thy grace we are confounded,
Holy, spotless Lamb of God.

When we see Thee, as the Victim,
Bound to the accursèd tree,
For our guilt and folly stricken,
All our judgment borne by Thee,
Lord, we own with hearts adoring,
Thou hast loved us unto blood:
Glory, glory everlasting,
Be to Thee, Thou Lamb of God!

This hymn is suited to the Lord's Supper. Its singing directs hearts in the footsteps of the Saviour—from the Father's bosom to the manger at Bethlehem, then to the garden of Gethsemane and onward to the tree at Golgotha. In its second part, the hymn traces further steps—upward to the throne and onward to millennial glory. Throughout, it seems as if each step on that unparalleled pathway is punctuated by the cry, "Behold, the Lamb of God!"

"I heard the voice of Jesus say"

Horatius Bonar (1808-1889)

Horatius Bonar.

Scotland, in the nineteenth century, was greatly influenced by the ministry of three brothers—John, Horatius and Andrew Bonar. Their father, James Bonar, was an Edinburgh lawyer, a man of great intellect and deep piety. Their mother was a spiritual woman who carefully and prayerfully guided the family after they were left fatherless at an early age. John, Horatius and Andrew were brought to Christ in their youth; they all became ministers of

[51

the gospel and were greatly used of the Lord throughout their native land.

Horatius was born on December 19th, 1808, in the city of Edinburgh and there he received his education, first at its High School and then at its University. In the course of his studies, Horatius came under the tutorship of Dr. Thomas Chalmers, a rugged Scot of steadfast character and genuine godliness and this spiritual giant exercised a tremendous influence for good in the life of his young student.

Bonar was ordained a minister of the Established Church in Scotland but later seceded at the "Disruption" in 1843. He had three scenes of ministry; first at Leith as assistant minister for three and a half years, then at Kelso in the Scottish Borders where he ministered for almost thirty years, and finally at Chalmer's Memorial Church in Edinburgh from 1866 until his death in 1889.

In Leith, Bonar was assistant to John Lewis of St. James' Church and there he laboured fervently, particularly among the youth of that poor, rough and needy district. During this period of life Bonar composed his first hymns; these were set to attractive tunes and used widely in his Sunday-school work as a replacement for the metrical version of the Psalms.

At Kelso, Bonar had a long and fruitful ministry. When he went there in 1837, as minister of the North Parish Church, a spiritual awakening was already sweeping through the country. Bonar gave himself wholeheartedly to the preaching of the gospel, proclaiming to crowded congregations in Kelso and beyond, the ever-needed truth, "Ye must be born again" (John 3:7); as a result many were saved under his ministry. In the year 1843, Bonar married Jane Catherine Lundie, whose father had been a minister in Kelso. She proved a congenial partner through life and is remembered today as the author of the lovely hymn, "Fade, fade each earthly joy; Jesus is mine".

Bonar's third and last ministerial charge was that of the Chalmer's Memorial Church in Edinburgh, following in the footsteps of his former tutor. He was well equipped for such a task and his Edinburgh years were fruitful for God. Then, after about seventeen years of busy ministry there, his health started to fail; a lingering illnes ensued and this compelled him to give up his active ministry. He remained undismayed in spirit right up to the last and through the closing years of life ever kept before him a lovely scripture text, "Until the day break, and the shadows flee away" (SoS. 2:17).

Bonar was a true Scot, strong in character and serious in manner. Nevertheless, he had a deep sense of humour and was very fond of children. He was a great scholar, well versed in English literature and particularly the classics; the ancient Greek and Latin hymns of the early church were of special interest to him. Above all, Horatius Bonar was a man of deep piety. "The light burned late in his study window and he was at his desk early. Members of his household heard his voice in prayer far into the night". One of his friends said of him that he was always praying, another that he was always visiting, another that he was always preaching and another that he was always writing.

Bonar wrote much. He was the author of hundreds of tracts. One of these, "Believe and Live" reached a circulation of one million copies and was a favourite with Queen Victoria. His books, *The Night of Weeping* and its sequel, *The Morning of Joy* with his devotional series, *God's Way of Peace* and *God's Way of Holiness* were greatly used of the Lord. As an acknowledgement of his literary contribution, the Aberdeen University conferred on him an honorary doctorate in 1853.

It is, however, for his verse that Horatius Bonar is best remembered; in fact he ranks as Scotland's most eminent hymn-writer. Some six hundred hymns have come from his pen and these first appeared in publication about the middle of the last century. *Hymns of Faith and Hope* (1857) is a fine collection of one hundred and fifteen of his best. John Ellerton has paid tribute to Bonar's influence in effecting, during his lifetime, a striking change in Scottish hymnody; he wrote, "The new wine of his *Hymns of Faith and Hope* has enriched the blood of all religious Scotland. Her heart grew hot within her and at last she spake with her tongue in new and freer accents of praise". Dr. John Julian's Dictionary says of Bonar's hymns that, "they win the heart by their tone of tender sympathy; they sing the truth of God in ringing notes." Indeed, an English lady has borne testimony, "that Horatius Bonar's hymns had nerved her when she was lagging in the race, cheered her in sorrow and trial, and kept her watching for the coming of the Lord."

The hymns of Horatius Bonar are intensely scriptural and often

deeply personal. They include hymns that give a clear vision of
Christ as Saviour, hymns that touch upon the blessedness of
communion at the Lord's supper and hymns that point onward to
the glorious hope of Christ's second advent. They are in essence
what Bonar termed them to be—*Hymns of Faith and Hope,* a
veritable treasure for the saints of God. In this rich collection may
be found such well-known favourites as,

"All that I was—my sin, my guilt"
"Blessed be God, our God!"
"Done is the work that saves"
"For the bread and for the wine"
"Go labour on; spend and be spent"
"Here, O my Lord, I see Thee face to face"
"I bless the Christ of God"
"I hear the words of love"
"I heard the voice of Jesus say"
"I was a wandering sheep"
"No blood, no altar now"
"When the weary, seeking rest"
"Yet there is room"

Bonar's hymn, "I heard the voice of Jesus say" is one of the
best-loved that have come from his pen. It was written during the
Kelso period of his ministry and first appeared in 1846 in *Hymns
Original and Selected.* When it was later included in the first series
of his *Hymns of Faith and Hope* (1857) it was entitled, "The Voice
from Galilee".

I heard the voice of Jesus say,
  "Come unto Me and rest;
Lay down, thou weary one, lay down
  Thy head upon My breast".
I came to Jesus as I was,
  Weary, and worn and sad;
I found in Him a resting-place,
  And He has made me glad.

I heard the voice of Jesus say,
*   "Behold I freely give*
The living water; thirsty one,
*   Stoop down, and drink, and live".*
I came to Jesus, and I drank
*   Of that life-giving stream;*
My thirst was quench'd, my soul revived,
*   And now I live in Him.*

I heard the voice of Jesus say,
*   "I am this dark world's light;*
Look unto Me, thy morn shall rise,
*   And all thy day be bright".*
I looked to Jesus, and I found,
*   In Him my Star, my Sun;*
And in that light of life I'll walk,
*   Till trav'lling days are done.*

This hymn tells out the experience of the child of God for the encouragement of the unconverted. There is in it a tender sympathy with the wants and aspirations of the human soul and this has welcomed the words to thousands of hearts. For the weary and burdened soul there is "rest"; for the spiritually thirsty there is "living water," and for the benighted traveller there is a "light" to guide and brighten the way. Every need is met abundantly in the Saviour.

In majestic greatness, "the Voice from Galilee" speaks to the souls of men at their point of need. His words of invitation and promise are for the weary, the thirsty and the lost. Horatius Bonar, in his youth, felt that he had been such. He had heard the call of "the Voice from Galilee" and had responded. In coming he had found rest and satisfaction for the heart, and in looking had found light and guidance for the way.

"Ten thousand times ten thousand"

Henry Alford (1810-1871)

Henry Alford.

"Some men have their memorial in stone; others in the hearts of those who have known and loved them; still others live on in the institutions they have founded and shaped. But among the most fortunate of mortals are those who remain contemporary by the continuing influence of their literary works. Such a man is Henry Alford". This, an introduction to Henry Alford by Dr. Everett F. Harrison immediately arouses our interest and increases our desire to know something further about this influential and interesting personality.

Henry Alford was born at 25 Alfred Place, Bedford Row, London on October 7th, 1810, the son of Henry Alford, an episcopal clergyman, the rector of Aston-Sandford. His mother died at his birth, and as an only child Henry received in early years all the attention and tender care that a devoted father could bestow.

He was a precocious child. When only six years of age, he outlined and illustrated a small book, *The Travels of St. Paul*. At the age of ten he wrote, *Looking unto Jesus, or the Believer's Support under Trials and Afflictions*. In his eleventh year there followed, *A Collection of Hymns for Sundry Occasions*. As a youth of sixteen, he entered in his Bible, "I do this day, as in the presence of God, and my own soul, renew my covenant with God, and solemnly determine henceforth to become His and do His work so far as in me lies", and throughout life Alford never deviated from that solemn intent.

Henry Alford at the age of seventeen enrolled at Trinity College, Cambridge and after an outstanding career there, graduated with honours in 1832; two years later he became a Fellow of the College. He entered the Church of England and following a two year period as curate in Ampton went on to become vicar at Wymeswold, Leicestershire and there he ministered for a period of eighteen years. He next moved to Quebec Chapel in London where for four years he exercised a notable ministry, his Sunday afternoon meetings there being oft-times frequented by members of Parliament, eminent lawyers and other distinguished intellectuals. In 1857, he was appointed by Lord Palmerston as Dean of Canterbury and there he remained until his death on January 12th, 1871. He is buried near to Canterbury Cathedral in St. Martin's Churchyard and on his tomb is inscribed the expressive epitaph (in Latin)

"THE INN OF A PILGRIM JOURNEYING TO JERUSALEM"

Henry Alford was a man of tremendous ability, one of the most gifted men of his day—a painter, a mechanic, a musician, a poet, a preacher, a scholar and a critic. "He was" remarks one contributor, "a man who could do anything and do it well". But it is his literary works which abide.

"His literary labours extend to every department of literature" declares James Davidson. He was an unwearying writer and published in all some fifty books, but by far his greatest work was his critical commentary on *The Greek Testament*. This, the product of more than twenty years labour, appears in four volumes and bears ample testimony to his outstanding scholarship. Of it, A. P. Stanley says, "It remains confessedly the best that exists in English of the whole volume of the New Testament".

The life and testimony of Henry Alford was beautified throughout by a delightful balance of love and truth. He loved all who loved His Lord. Besides, he dearly loved the truth of God and declared it with firmness, yet in a meek and quiet spirit. Once in his university days after completing the reading of his New Testament he wrote in his journal, "Always estimate men in proportion as they estimate this Book". Some thirty years later he wrote again, "I am fully prepared, however unworthy, to cast in my lot among those who are digging in the soil of Scripture for the precious truth that lies beneath". The Word of God was his daily bread and oft-times at the end of a day's study he would close his books, stand up and give God thanks for spiritual food. He acknowledged God in all his ways and laboured unsparingly as one convinced that God had a work for him to do.

Henry Alford was a notable hymn-writer and besides composing hymns translated others from their original languages. He compiled several collections of hymns, and in his *Year of Praise*, appearing first in 1867, there were no fewer than fifty-five hymns of his own composition. Millar Patrick's judgment of Alford's hymns is that they are, "like glowing coals brought from the altar of a soul whose whole joy was worship". Oft-times the product of a soaring spirit engaged with some heavenly theme, the expression is rich and majestic, firing the soul. The deep sorrow of bereavement that crossed his path in the year 1866 led to one of his finest hymns,

> *Ten thousand times ten thousand,*
> *In sparkling raiment bright,*
> *The armies of the ransomed saints*
> *Throng up the steeps of light;*

'Tis finished, all is finished,
  Their fight with death and sin;
Fling open wide the golden gates,
  And let the victors in.

What rush of hallelujahs
  Fills all the earth and sky!
What ringing of a thousand harps
  Bespeaks the triumph nigh!
O day for which creation
  And all its tribes were made!
O joy, for all its former woes
  A thousand-fold repaid!

O then what raptured greetings
  On Canaan's happy shore,
What knitting severed friendships up
  Where partings are no more!
Then eyes with joy shall sparkle
  That brimmed with tears of late;
Orphans no longer fatherless,
  Nor widows desolate.

Bring near thy great salvation,
  Thou Lamb for sinners slain:
Fill up the roll of Thine elect,
  Then take Thy power and reign;
Appear, Desire of nations—
  Thine exiles long for home;
Show in the heaven Thy promised sign;
  Thou Prince and Saviour, come!

The return of the Lord Jesus our "Prince and Saviour" will be glorious! It is recorded of King Charles II that, at the outbreak of the great plague of London, he fled in terror from the stricken city to Hampton Court and took his treasures with him. Though the pestilence raged within the city and many died, he showed no concern; he sent no contribution to the Relief Fund. When the ravages of the plague were past, the King turned again towards his London palace, heralds riding on before to announce his coming.

The people, however, on hearing the announcement retired within their homes, closed the doors and shutters and left the streets utterly deserted. As reports of such desolation filtered back to the approaching King, he was filled with shame and turned back again to Hampton Court. There he awaited the hours of darkness and then secretly crept back through the deserted streets to his London palace. In all his journey, there was not one soul to greet him.

It will not be so at the return of the Lord Jesus. Alford in his hymn anticipates that great event and catches something of the atmosphere of that glorious day. Then countless armies of redeemed will gather on Canaan's happy shore, then every exile will be home at last and painful partings all forgotten in blessed reunion. Tear-dimmed eyes will sparkle once again and a rush of hallelujahs fill both earth and sky as the day of Calvary's ultimate triumph o'er every issue of the fall be ushered in. Towards that great consummation everything presently is marching on; all creation waits for it; every redeemed soul longs for it, and Henry Alford within his heart, felt that it could not come too soon.

"There is life for a look at the Crucified One"

Amelia Matilda Hull (1812-?1882)

Marpool Hall, Exmouth.
(Where Amelia M. Hull wrote "There is life for a look").

"Not many noble ("high-born"—J.N.D.) are called" (I Cor. 1:26); and yet, in sovereign grace, God sometimes visits such families with His salvation. In the last century, the Hulls of South Devon were a shining example of such Divine intervention. They were a noble family of renowned military tradition and lived at Marpool Hall on the outskirts of Exmouth, and though today their ancient family home has disappeared and been replaced by a public park (Phear Park), yet still there remains in that part of England very fragrant memories of the Hulls of Marpool Hall.

Anna (Amelia) Matilda Hull was born on September 30th, 1812, the youngest of a family of eleven children of William Thomas and Harriott Hull of Marpool Hall. Her father was a retired army captain. Of Amelia's personal life, very little has been left on record apart from the story of her conversion. However, the circumstances of that great event are so full of interest and are so inextricably linked with the birth of her lovely hymn, "There is life for a look at the Crucified One" that they are worth relating.

It has been recorded that when Amelia was about twenty years of age she heard the gospel of Christ for the first time. A visiting evangelist had pitched his tent near to their family home and invited the neighbouring people to come and hear the gospel. One night Amelia ventured to go. She slipped in at the back of the tent and listened with intent to the gospel of Jesus Christ. Her heart was troubled. When she returned home and told her father where she had been, he was furious. He told her that association with such "ranters" and their meetings was not becoming to anyone in her station of life, and he forbade her to go back. However, Amelia's heart had already received the first droppings of the living water and she thirsted for more. She felt she must go back and in spite of her father's forbidding, she returned the following evening. The message on that occasion was taken from John 3:14,15, "And as Moses lifted up the serpent in the wilderness, even so must the Son of man be lifted up: that whosoever believeth in Him should not perish, but have eternal life". In that meeting Amelia looked by faith to the Christ of Calvary and was saved for eternity.

On her arrival home, she met with her father's fury. He was beside himself with rage. Taking her to the library he scolded her severely for what she had done and ordered that she appear there again next morning at 9 o'clock to be horse-whipped. With mixed feelings, Amelia retired for the night: having incurred her father's displeasure she was sad, and yet the deep joy of God's salvation filled and flooded her soul. She thought upon the events of the past evening—upon the greatness of the message which had brought her peace and, as she did so, she jotted down her heart's musings upon a piece of paper. When 9 o'clock arrived, she made her way to the library with the piece of paper in her hand. There stood her father; his riding-whip lay upon the table. She entered, handed him the piece of paper and waited. Captain William Thomas Hull stood there that morning and read the words of Amelia's composition:

> *There is life for a look at the Crucified One,*
> *There is life at this moment for thee;*
> *Then look, sinner, look unto Him and be saved,*
> *Unto Him who was nailed to the tree.*
>
> *Oh, why was He there as the Bearer of sin,*
> *If on Jesus thy guilt was not laid?*
> *Oh, why from His side flowed the sin-cleansing Blood,*
> *If His dying thy debt has not paid?*
>
> *It is not thy tears of repentance or prayers,*
> *But the Blood, that atones for the soul;*
> *On Him, then Who shed it, thou mayest at once*
> *Thy weight of iniquities roll.*
>
> *Then doubt not thy welcome, since God has declared*
> *There remaineth no more to be done;*
> *That once in the end of the world He appeared,*
> *And completed the work He begun.*
>
> *Then take with rejoicing from Jesus at once*
> *The Life Everlasting He gives;*
> *And know with assurance thou never canst die,*
> *Since Jesus, thy righteousness, lives.*

As he read, a change came over him. He sat down and buried his face in his hands. God had spoken to his heart and he was now a broken man. Gone was any thought of horse-whipping his daughter. Instead, in the library that morning, Captain Hull sought and found his daughter Amelia's Saviour.

From that day forward, a great tranformation was effected both in the Captain's personal life and in every-day life at Marpool Hall. He had become a new creature in Christ Jesus and Marpool Hall became a Christian home. Several other members of the family experienced the same saving change and led lives wholly devoted to the service of God. Through the influence of the Hull family, a hall on the Exeter Road was acquired for the preaching of the gospel and in 1843 a private cemetery was secured at Withycombe, to be used exclusively for the burial of believers who had been in assembly fellowship. Five of the eleven members of that notable Hull family have been laid to rest in that little cemetery. Truly the miracle of God's salvation wrought unprecedented change in that illustrious family of South Devon.

Amelia's lovely hymn, penned on the night of her conversion, has been blessed by God to countless hearts. The verses are marked by a great simplicity and an amazing clarity. Nevertheless, they express tremendous spiritual truth—truth which again and again has been used by the Spirit of God to help sin-burdened souls find the way of salvation. By these words, Amelia Hull sweetly draws seeking souls to the cross of Christ. That cross becomes precious; it becomes everything. How assuredly she speaks to hearts there! There all arguments are silenced; there all questionings cease; there all human endeavour is abandoned, for the Saviour's work is so totally sufficient for the soul's salvation. Sin's load has been completely borne. Sin's debt has been fully paid. Full atonement has been made at inestimable cost, and salvation's work for sinful man stands perfect and complete. What Divine provision for worthless creatures!—and all that has been procured there on that cross by the Infinite Sufferer may be secured personally by the sinner through "a look of faith".

Oh the immensity, the finality and the sufficiency of the Saviour's sacrifice! It meets the sinner's need in full and forever...but, if not, then Calvary must forever remain the supreme tragedy of all history, the great mystery of all ages.

> Oh, why was He there as the Bearer of sin,
>   If on Jesus thy guilt was not laid?
> Oh, why from His side flowed the sin-cleansing Blood,
>   If His dying thy debt has not paid?

"O blessed Lord,
what hast Thou done!"

Mary Peters (1813-1856)

Tombstone of Mary Peters.
(Arnos Vale, Bristol).

Mary Peters (née Bowly) was born in Cirencester, Gloucestershire, England on April 17th, 1813, the sixth in the family of seven
children of Richard and Mary Bowly. Her father was a liner draper
by trade and a member of a well-known and highly respected
Quaker family in that ancient Cotswold town. Mary was a talented
girl and devoted much of her time to the study of history. As a

165

consequence of that early interest and application, she published a most ambitious literary work *The World's History from the Creation to the Accession of Queen Victoria*, (alternatively entitled, *Universal History in Scripture Principles*); throughout the seven volumes of that prodigious work, Mary traced the hand of God in all the great events of this world's history.

Mary's spiritual life in its early years was lived worthy of her Lord and in close communion with Him. In those days, a great spiritual movement had begun in the part of England where she lived and its influence was to further mould and enrich her life for God. Men and women, convicted and convinced by the simple teaching of God's Word, dissociated themselves from the Established Churches around them and gathered simply to the Name of the Lord Jesus. It is recorded that George Müller, one of outstanding teachers of that early movement, came to Nailsworth, some ten miles from Mary's home, in 1841 and there spent six weeks "labouring in the Word among the saints". It was very probably under this ministry that Mary imbibed some of the precious Scripture truths that later appeared, skilfully woven into her hymns.

At the age of thirty-nine, Mary married John William Peters, M.A., "a minister of the gospel at Quenington, Gloucestershire". Peters in earlier years had been rector of the Established Church in Quenington and vicar of Langford, but there came a time in his ministry when he was no longer happy to continue with certain teachings and practices of the Church to which he belonged. He thereupon graciously resigned his "living" and built a simple little chapel in Quenington for the preaching of the gospel. That building bore no distinctive name and included within it a baptistry for the baptism by immersion of those who were believers in the Lord Jesus.

John W. Peters had been widowed for some six years when he married Mary Bowly, on April 13th, 1852. The marriage took place in Cirencester and the ceremony was conducted by Mr. George Müller. Very shortly afterwards, John and Mary moved from Quenington to Clifton in Bristol. There they spent four brief but happy years together until Mary's death on July 29th, 1856, at the early age of forty-three. She was buried in Arnos Vale Cemetery, Bristol and the burial service was conducted by Mr. Henry Craik.

Mary was a talented hymn-writer. She wrote most of her compositions when still single and while living in Circencester. The suggestion, by some commentators, of an early widowhood being the background to some of her verse (as "faith can sing through days of sorrow, All, all is well") appears to be without foundation. She wrote in all some fifty-eight hymns and most of these were published collectively in 1847 as *Hymns Intended to Help the Communion of Saints.*

Mary Peters' hymns today still hold a place of prominence among believers gathered to the Name of the Lord Jesus. The present edition of *The Believer's Hymn Book* contains some twelve that have come from her pen.

> "Around Thy table, Holy Lord"
> "Blessed Lord, our souls are longing"
> "Lord Jesus, in Thy name alone"
> "O blessed Lord, what hast Thou done!"
> "O Lord, how much Thy name unfolds"
> "Of Thee, Lord, we would never tire"
> "Praise ye the Lord, again, again"
> "Salvation to our God"
> "The holiest now we enter"
> "Through the love of God our Saviour"
> "'Tis we, O Lord, whom Thou hast shown"
> "Unworthy our thanksgiving"

These hymns of Mary Peters, packed with scriptural content, are to edification and breathe the very air of Heaven. They both confirm the faith of the child of God and exalt the precious person of the Lord Jesus. The believer's past, his present, and his glorious future come within the sweep of her pen but her chief extolling theme is the person of her glorious Lord—His fragrant Name, His precious blood, His faithful priesthood and His intrinsic personal and eternal worth. She borrows freely from Old Testament typology and weaves it in a masterly way into her verse and thus the theme of her pen takes on new and added lustre. Perhaps her loveliest on the person of the Saviour is "Whom have we Lord, but Thee" (not included in the Believer's Hymn Book collection).

Whom have we, Lord, but Thee,
  Soul thirst to satisfy?
Exhaustless spring! The waters free!
  All other streams are dry.

Her hymn "O blessed Lord, what hast Thou done!" is familiar to many and very sweet; its sublime theme is the greatness of what God has done.

O blessed Lord, what hast Thou done!
  How vast a ransom paid!
God's only well-beloved Son
  Upon the altar laid!

The Father, in His willing love,
  Could spare Thee from His side;
And Thou couldst stoop, to bear above,
  At such a cost, Thy Bride.

While our full hearts in faith repose
  Upon Thy precious blood,
Peace in a steady current flows,
  Filled from Thy mercy's flood.

What boundless joy will fill each heart,
  Our every grief efface,
When we behold Thee as Thou art
  And all Thy love retrace.

Unseen we love Thee, dear Thy Name!
  But when our eyes behold,
With joyful wonder we'll proclaim
  The half hath not been told!

In this hymn, Mary Peters again borrows truth from the Old Testament to magnify her theme. Types are introduced to advantage. In the background there are Abraham and Isaac upon the mount in the land of Moriah; there is Jacob serving for Rachel in Padanaram and there is the Queen of Sheba on her visit to King Solomon in Jerusalem. In every case, the type is outstripped and eclipsed. The earthly father and son upon the mount recede from our gaze and we see only the heavenly; all the years of humiliation and patient service of a Jacob seem as nothing in light of the securing cost of the bride of Christ, and the words of wonder of the Queen of Sheba are but a faint whisper of the full and final exclamation of redeemed and adoring hearts, "the half hath not been told!"

"When this passing world is done"

Robert Murray McCheyne (1813-1843)

Robert Murray McCheyne.

"There has been one among us who ere he had reached the age at which a priest in Israel would have been entering on his course, dwelt at the Mercy-seat as if it were his home—preached the certainties of eternal life with an undoubting mind—and spent his nights and days in ceaseless breathings after holiness, and the salvation of sinners. Hundreds of souls were his reward from the Lord, ere he left us; and in him have we been taught how much one man may do who will only press further into the presence of his

170

God, and handle more skilfully the unsearchable riches of Christ, and speak more boldly for his God." This tribute to Robert Murray McCheyne from the pen of his intimate friend and biographer, Dr. Andrew Bonar, has been taken from his memoir. "Read McCheyne's memoir", urged Mr. Spurgeon, "read the whole of it ... it is the story of the life of a man who walked with God."

Robert Murray McCheyne was born May 21st, 1813 in the city of Edinburgh and there he spent his early years—at home, at high school and at university.

The year, 1831 was for Robert a time of spiritual crisis. He was then eighteen years of age. The circumstances surrounded the unexpected death of his brother David who was eight years his senior. The two brothers were deeply attached and in David's death, Robert sustained a tremendous loss. Later he wrote, "this dear friend and brother died ... I found the misery of being friendless. I do not mean that I had no relatives or worldly friends for I had many, but I had no friend who cared for my soul. I had none to direct me to the Saviour ... " Whether this bereavement was the time of Robert's awakening or the time of his salvation, or perhaps both, we cannot be certain but we know that afterwards, Robert ever kept the anniversary as sacred. On each July 8th, reference was made to it in his journal, and in 1842, the closing year of his life, he made the entry, "This day eleven years ago I lost my loved and loving brother and began to seek a Brother who cannot die".

In the winter of the same year, 1831, Robert commenced his studies for the ministry in Edinburgh under Dr. Chalmers and Dr. Welsh. At college he continued for a time to indulge in worldy pursuits, though with growing alarm of conscience. That he was the object of Divine grace captivated his thoughts, "Truly there was nothing in me that should have induced Him to choose me. I was but as other brands, upon whom the fire is already kindled and shall burn for evermore!" He perused the memoirs of Henry Martyn and longed that he might become like him. "Would I could imitate him, giving up father and mother, country, house, health, life, all—for Christ. And yet, what hinders? Lord, purify me and give me strength to dedicate myself, my all to Thee!"

Earth's broken cisterns became to McCheyne as nothing compared with the Fountain of living waters. He turned his back upon the world but soon found that in himself there was a world of pollution, a cesspool of corruption. In his dilemma he read and pondered the life of David Brainerd, of that youth possessed of an inward loathing of and struggle against sin. McCheyne longed for holiness. He was convinced, "It is not talents God blesses so much as great likeness to Jesus . . . Unholiness lies at the root of our little success". In the presence of God he poured out his deepest longing, "Lord, make me as holy as a pardoned sinner can be made". Thus, at nineteen years of age, he set his sails and God acknowledged and accepted that earnest resolve.

McCheyne, at that time, had a great desire for foreign missionary work. He conferred with his tutor, Dr. Chalmers, who advised him to seek experience first among the slums of Edinburgh. He adopted the suggestion and there, for a time, saw something of human need.

At the early age of twenty-three, McCheyne was called as minister to St. Peter's in Dundee. In the Divine plan for his life, God had allotted to him only six more years; these he gave to Dundee and each one was full for God. The first three were years of ploughing and sowing; the last three were years of abundant reaping.

When McCheyne went to Dundee in 1836, he found it to be a hardened and godless city given over to idolatry and drunkenness. His charge was a large parish of some four thousand souls, many of whom had never crossed the threshold of any church. McCheyne, as one convinced that his time there would be short, gave himself unsparingly to the work. He laboured fervently night and day, and laboured in faith, "Perhaps the Lord will have this wilderness of chimney-tops to be green and beautiful as the garden of the Lord, a field which the Lord hath blessed".

Initially the field proved arid and barren; nothing appeared for God. After three years of diligent toil his health gave way and he was forced to have a complete break. In company with a group of godly Scottish ministers he set out on the Commission to Jews in Palestine and Eastern Europe. This proved to be part of the Divine plan and God mightily blessed that work. Many Jews were saved as the result, among them noteworthies as Adolph Saphir and Alfred Edersheim.

In the meantime, back in Dundee, the spiritual harvest had begun and many seeking souls were daily finding the Saviour.

McCheyne, on hearing of this Divine visitation, longed to be back among his own people. He returned and saw for himself that great work of the Spirit of God. The windows of Heaven had been opened and the hitherto arid and barren wilderness was bringing forth abundantly. For three years McCheyne reaped of that abundant harvest. Then, at the early age of twenty-nine, he graciously laid down his sickle; his days of service were complete. In the early hours of Saturday, March 25th 1843, after a brief illness, he took leave of his parishioners, of the city of Dundee, and of this world. Oft he had exhorted his hearers, "Live so as to be missed", and, at his passing a voice of weeping was heard in almost every household; strong men were bowed in grief, the city was steeped in mourning. Thus McCheyne's ministry in the city of Dundee was brought to an abrupt ending: though short, it had been powerful, fruitful, unforgettable. But what was the secret?

The secret! Dr. F. W. Boreham says, "It was simply this; he walked with God . . . It was in rapt communion with the unseen that he became infected with his Master's insatiable hunger for the souls of men. He wept over Dundee as Jesus wept over Jerusalem". Mrs. Andrew Bonar spake of him, "It was neither his matter nor his manner that struck me; it was the impression of his likeness to Christ—a picture so lovely that I felt I would have given all the world to be as he was!" As he walked with God, so he talked with God. When he prayed, he seemed to be standing in the immediate presence of the Most High, looking into the very eyes of God and talking with Him face to face. And thus, from the Divine presence, he came forth to pour out his heart to the people. He was, among them, a true pastor, a shepherd who felt he must give account for each one.

Robert Murray McCheyne has left for succeeding generations an example and a legacy—an example to be emulated, a legacy to be treasured. A valuable collection of his hymns and poems form part of that treasured legacy and his compositions make a warm appeal to every true child of God. Two in particular are specially loved—"I once was a stranger to grace and to God", an account in verse of his own spiritual experience, and "When this passing world is done". The latter was written during his first year in Dundee. It was entitled, "I am debtor" and in its original had nine verses.

When this passing world is done,
  When has sunk yon glaring sun,
When I stand with Christ in glory,
  Looking o'er life's finished story,
Then, Lord, shall I fully know—
  Not 'till then—how much I owe.

Robert Murray McCheyne was convinced that this world was passing. He did not become entangled. He lived for another world.

"Rise, my soul! behold 'tis Jesus

Joseph Denham Smith (1817-1889)

Joseph Denham Smith.

In early September 1857 four young converts met to pray in an old school house near to the village of Kells in the parish of Connor, Co. Antrim, Ireland. The burden of their hearts was for a work of the Spirit of God throughout the land. Fervent intercessions were made weekly by these young men, but all through the succeeding months their cries to God seemed in vain. Then, on January 1st, 1858, God opened the windows of Heaven—first the droppings, then the showers, then the outpourings of blessing, until the land, which

175

hitherto had been arid and barren, was in spiritual flood. God had heard, God had answered and a great spiritual awakening and revival swept throughout the North of Ireland.

Joseph Denham Smith was an instrument of God in that great spiritual harvest. At the time of its commencement, he was pastor of a Congregational Church in Kingstown (Dun Laoghaire) outside the city of Dublin. He had been born in England (July, 1817) at Romsey, Hants, and there he had spent his early years. He had known the devoted care and guidance of a widowed mother whose one desire for her boy was that early in life he might come to know the Saviour. God had abundantly answered that mother's prayer—Joseph had been led to Christ and soon afterwards had devoted his life to the work of the Lord. On hearing of Ireland's deep spiritual need, he moved to the city of Dublin and, after studying at its Theological Institute, he entered the Congregational ministry. His first charge was in the town of Newry, Co. Down and in 1848 he moved to Kingstown as pastor of a newly established Congregational Church in Northumberland Avenue.

In August, 1859, Denham Smith had a visit from a Mr. and Mrs. Morley of Clapton. They had come from London to see something of the beauties of the Wicklow mountains and were about to return home. "But you will not return, will you, without seeing something of the remarkable revival?" remarked their host. So, together with the Morleys, Denham Smith travelled north, and in the city of Belfast and in County Antrim he witnessed personally something of that great movement of the Spirit of God—souls, in their hundreds, smitten down by a deep sense of their own sin and guilt and awakened to the reality of coming judgment were crying out aloud to God for His mercy; many were finding salvation and peace in the Lord Jesus. Denham Smith was deeply moved by what he witnessed. He was convinced that it was a work of God.

The great revival of 1859, as a surging flood and as a spreading flame, reached the city of Dublin and district by early September of the same year. Joseph Denham Smith wholeheartedly entered into the movement. Leaving Kingstown, he moved centrally to the city of Dublin and there gave himself unreservedly to the proclamation of the gospel and the helping of troubled souls. Through the influence of Mr. William Fry, a well-known and highly-respected Dublin solicitor, the old Metropolitan Hall in Lower Abbey Street was acquired as a centre of meeting and there, "thousands flocked together in the morning, and remained hour after hour, many without refreshments—until ten and eleven at night. Careless ones were awakened, anxious ones led into peace, and persons of all classes rejoiced in a newly-found Saviour."

The city of Dublin was touched in no small way by the '59 revival; the human instrument at the centre of the movement was Joseph Denham Smith. An article, recounting his life and work, bears witness to the richness of that spiritual harvest in Ireland's capital city—"conversion invariably attends the services; as few as one and as many as sixty-nine have been reported as the result of a single meeting; and on the anniversary of the outbreak of the work, it was announced that some three thousand known conversions had resulted in the space of twelve months. Many of the conversions have been of a remarkable kind. Roman Catholics of all classes, including the highest ladies and gentlemen moving in the best circles in Dublin, young men and women from the shops and warehouses, sailors, soldiers, and children of tender age have alike professed change of heart and have manifested that change in their life". Among those who were saved at that time through the instrumentality of Denham Smith was Shuldham Henry who afterwards was greatly used of the Lord in the work of the gospel.

The time came when Denham Smith felt that he could no longer be bound by denominational ties. He thereupon resigned from the pastorate of Kingstown and sought to serve his Lord in the preaching of the gospel and in a ministry to His people without denominational distinction. A more suitable and permanent meeting place was called for, as a centre from which Denham Smith might carry on this work in Dublin. No suitable building was available; so it was decided to erect a new one. After acquisition of a site near to Merrion Square, a building with a capacity for two thousand, five hundred people was planned and building commenced in 1862. Merrion Hall was opened the following year and for over a century was a great gathering centre for the preaching of the gospel and later became the home of the assembly of the Lord's people. Down the years many noted and devoted servants of Christ have occupied its platform with attendant refreshment and blessing from the presence of the Lord. Such household names as Richard Weaver, Grattan Guinness, Shuldham Henry, Harry Moorehouse, George Müller and Dr. Barnardo are numbered among those early labourers but, perhaps, none have been more closely linked nor have seen more abundant blessing in

Merrion Hall than Joseph Denham Smith. He personally played a leading role in its institution, was present at its opening, saw fruitful blessing there in the early years of its history and throughout his life-time maintained a close link with the assembly meeting there.

Denham Smith, in his labours, travelled to the continent of Europe and in the capital cities of Paris and Geneva ministered the precious Word of God to large gatherings of both saved and unsaved. He visited the city of London and there, in later years, he made his home from which he continued in active service for the Lord. His health, however, started to fail ere he had reached his seventieth birthday and on March 5th, 1889, at the age of seventy-one, he passed away peacefully into the presence of his Lord.

Joseph Denham Smith left behind a fragrant memory. Those who knew him were deeply impressed by his devotion to Christ. His ministries, extending over a period of more than fifty years, were always replete with the savour of Christ. From the very first when, as a lad of sixteen, he commenced to preach, right to the close, Christ was ever his central theme. In his preaching, his style was eloquent, yet simple, his powers of language and illustration exceeded only by the power of the accompanying Spirit of God. His written ministry too, reflects his deep devotion to his Lord and among his known publications are such gems as, *The Gospel in Hosea, The Brides of Scripture* and *Green Pastures*.

As a hymn-writer, Denham Smith produced compositions which were both scriptural and sweet. These first received publication in periodicals throughout the latter half of the last century. He compiled a volume of hymns, *Hymns for General and Special Use* and in this there appeared no fewer than thirty-six, signed as written by himself. Among his compositions there are to be found such well-known favourites as:

> "God's Almighty arms are round me"
> "Jesus, Thy dying love I own"
> "Just as Thou art—how wondrous fair"
> "My God, I have found"
> "Rise, my soul! behold 'tis Jesus"

This last mentioned is a great favourite with many at the Lord's supper:

Rise, my soul! behold 'tis Jesus,
  Jesus fills thy wond'ring eyes;
See Him now in glory seated,
  Where thy sins no more can rise.

There, in righteousness transcendent,
  Lo! He doth in heaven appear,
Shows the blood of His atonement
  As thy title to be there.

All thy sins were laid upon Him,
  Jesus bore them on the tree;
God who knew them, laid them on Him,
  And, believing, thou art free.

God now brings thee to His dwelling,
  Spreads for thee His feast divine;
Bids thee welcome, ever telling
  What a portion there is thine.

In that circle of God's favour,
  Circle of the Father's love;
All is rest, and rest for ever,
  All is perfectness above.

Blessèd glorious word "forever"!
  Yea, "forever" is the word;
Nothing can the ransomed sever,
  Naught divide them from the Lord.

A look within the heavenly sanctuary both stirs and stills the heart.
There the Saviour sits in glory, and there irrefutable evidences
abound of the sufficiency of His work for our salvation. The impact
of such majestic and assuring sights first bids our souls to rise, then
beckons them to rest.

"There is a green hill far away"

Cecil Frances Alexander (1818-1895)

Cecil Frances Alexander.

Among the best-known and best-loved of women hymn-writers of the last century were "The Three Fannys"—Fanny Crosby, the blind poetess of North America, Fanny Havergal, the sweet singer of England, and Fanny Alexander, linked exclusively with Ireland. On this beautiful emerald isle Mrs. Alexander spent her days, commencing them in the capital city of Dublin and concluding them in the maiden city of Londonderry. Among renowned Irish poets and hymn-writers, Mrs. Cecil Frances Alexander (C.F.A.) takes a foremost place; she is, in fact, one of Ireland's famous daughters.

Frances was the second daughter of Major John and Mrs. Humphreys and was born at 25 Eccles Street, Dublin in 1818.* Her childhood and early youth were spent in that part of Ireland, first in Dublin city and then at Ballykeane House in County Wicklow. When only a girl, Frances started to write little poems and stow them away, sometimes under the carpet; her father, on discovering these discerned that they were the product of unusual talent and thereafter sought to give encouragement to his daughter in her compositions in every possible way.

When Frances was fifteen the family moved to Milltown House, Strabane, in County Tyrone. For Frances this was but the first of many homes in the North-West of Ireland, and at Milltown House she lived with her family until her marriage in 1850. During these years Frances kept busy with her pen, writing hymns mostly for children. These compositions, perhaps the finest of all her works in verse, were published as *Hymns for Little Children* in 1848. The preface to this valuable collection was written by John Keble and the volume was dedicated to Frances' godsons.

Frances' godsons were a group of Sunday-school children in Strabane who had been experiencing great difficulty in memorizing the Church Catechism and Apostles' Creed; the words and phrases were so difficult to understand that their labour had become dull and dreary. Then Frances, appreciating their difficulty, set herself to write simple verse to explain the words of the Creed and then this hitherto boring subject became full of interest and delight.

Frances wrote the simple hymn, "All things bright and beautiful" to explain the words of the Creed, "I believe in God, the Father Almighty, Maker of heaven and earth". Her well-known children's hymn, "Once in Royal David's city" gave fresh meaning to the words, "and in Jesus Christ, His only Son, our Lord, who was conceived of the Holy Ghost, born of the virgin Mary". Then when the children should have repeated the words of the Creed "suffered under Pontius Pilate, was crucified, dead and buried", she got them to sing instead, "There is a green hill far away". In this way Frances produced some of the greatest hymns ever written for children.

In 1850, Frances married William Alexander, the rector of Termonamongan, County Tyrone, "a parish in a wild area scattered over bogs and mountains for many miles." There the Alexanders

*sometimes given as 1823

spent their first five years of married life residing at Derg Lodge, and, while her husband ministered at St. Bestius Church near Killeter, Frances busied herself in attending to the needs of the sick, aged and lonely in that poor and desolate parish. The old parish clerk referred to her as "the lady who went with comforts for the sick and sorrowful in all weathers when it was not fit for the likes of her to be out" and "many a gleam of golden sunshine would she kindle as she entered a desolate home where penury and sickness struggled for the mastery . . . The good she did, the help afforded, her gentle, loving self-effacing ministry in this parish will never be known 'until the day break and the shadows flee away'."

In 1855 the Alexanders moved to the parish of Upper Fahan in County Donegal on the shores of beautiful Lough Swilly ("the lake of shadows"). There they made their home at the glebehouse, her husband ministering in the nearby St. Mura's Parish Church and Frances keeping busy with her practical ministries and pen as aforetime. After five years they returned again to County Tyrone, Dr. Alexander having been appointed rector of Christ Church, Strabane. During these years they lived at Camus Rectory on the river Mourne and there, on many a pleasant summer evening, Frances would have been seen sitting outside her home playing on her Irish harp.

In 1867, Dr. Alexander was appointed Bishop of Londonderry and Raphoe and the family then moved to the Bishop's Palace, Bishop Street, Londonderry. Though now moving in higher social circles, Frances never deviated from her humble and sacrificial ministries, visiting lowly homes in the back streets of the city and helping in the "Home for Fallen Women".

On October 12th, 1895, at the age of seventy-seven, Frances' beautiful life came to a close and, "she was laid in her grave amidst the tears of a great community" in the City Cemetery, Londonderry, sited on a green hill, just outside the city wall.

During her lifetime, Mrs. Cecil Frances Alexander wrote and published some four hundred hymns and poems. These appeared in several volumes about the middle of the last century but after her death the best of her work was collected by her husband and compiled as a single volume, *Poems of Cecil Frances Alexander*; in its preface Dr. Alexander said this, "To the writer the thought often occurs that these eternal words, rising day after day from myriads of human souls form themselves into a continual memorial of her before

God. The memorial will continue, for the preacher's influence is of a few years, the hymnist's is of all time".

So, across the continents and through the years, a memorial to Mrs. Cecil Frances Alexander has continued through the singing of her lovely hymns; but, of all her compositions, none perhaps is more sweet or better loved than her simple children's hymn, "There is a green hill far away".

> *There is a green hill far away,*
>   *Without a city wall,*
> *Where the dear Lord was crucified*
>   *Who died to save us all.*

> *We may not know, we cannot tell*
>   *What pains He had to bear;*
> *But we believe it was for us*
>   *He hung and suffered there.*

> *He died that we might be forgiven,*
>   *He died to make us good,*
> *That we might go at last to heaven,*
>   *Saved by His precious blood.*

> *There was no other good enough*
>   *To pay the price of sin;*
> *He only could unlock the gate*
>   *Of heaven, and let us in.*

> *Oh, dearly, dearly has He loved,*
>   *And we must love Him too,*
> *And trust in His redeeming blood,*
>   *And try His works to do.*

This hymn was written by Frances in 1847 as she sat by the bedside of a sick child who afterwards always referred to it as "her hymn". The words first appeared in print the following year in *Hymns for Little Children* and were entitled, "Good Friday". Charles Gounod, the famous French composer, set them to music and considered it, "the most beautiful hymn in the English Language".

In the opening line of this beautiful hymn Mrs. Alexander brings us to Calvary and, in the simplest and clearest of language, speak to our hearts of the greatness of what was enacted there—it was our salvation. The suffering entailed was beyond human comprehension; the cost involved was beyond human computation. Only One had sufficient resources to meet such needs; in love that One gave His all—He paid the price in full, He unlocked the gate of Heaven and procured for the sinner a fitness to be there.

"What a Friend we have in Jesus"

Joseph Medlicott Scriven (1819-1886)

Joseph Medlicott Scriven.

"Poets learn in suffering what they teach in song"; such a truth is amply illustrated from the circumstances surrounding the writing of this well-loved hymn, "What a Friend we have in Jesus".

Joseph Medlicott Scriven, the author of this hymn, was born on September 10th, 1819, at Ballymoney Lodge, Banbridge, in County Down, Ireland. He was the third and youngest son of Captain John

185

and Jane (née Medlicott) Scriven. Captain John Scriven had ambitions and plans for Joseph's life—that he should train for a military career and thereafter serve his country; God had other plans.

Joseph went to study at Trinity College, Dublin and while there he came into contact with the gospel. He discovered that he needed a personal Saviour and found in the Lord Jesus one who was sufficient to meet his need. This experience of conversion changed completely the whole outlook and course of Joseph's life.

He graduated B.A. from Trinity in 1842. In the same year he was engaged to be married and life then held for him promise of much happiness. His marriage was arranged for the summer of 1844 but just on the eve of the wedding-day, his sweetheart was accidentally drowned in the River Bann.

Joseph then decided to make a fresh start in life and in the following year he emigrated to Canada and settled around the borders of Lake Ontario where, for a time, he taught school and acted as a private tutor. In that district of Canada he gave himself to evangelistic and philanthropic work, preaching the gospel to crowds at fairs and markets and working untiringly for the poor and afflicted. Among the local people he became known as, "the man who saws wood and carries water for sick people and widows unable to pay".

In those years another severe trial crossed his pathway. His second sweetheart, Eliza Roche, the neice of a Captain Pengally fell sick following a chill. Three years of lingering illness ensued and during that time Scriven stayed much by his fiancée's bedside and helped with her nursing care, but in spite of all medical effort Eliza's condition slowly deteriorated and she died. Her much-wasted body was laid to rest in a small hillside cemetery overlooking Rice Lake, just outside Bewdley in Ontario.

Following this an indescribable grief filled Scriven's heart and for the remainder of his life he seemed to carry with him a secret sorrow. His path, though dark, was one of close fellowship with God; the seeming tragedies of his life rather than bringing in their train bitterness and hardness of spirit, served only to make his devotion to Christ more intense and more sweet. The dark clouds surrounding his path had moreover a beautiful silver lining and out of the tragic experience surrounding Eliza's death in the year 1857, there was born in Scriven's heart one of the sweetest hymns known today in the English language:

What a Friend we have in Jesus,
All our sins and griefs to bear!
What a privilege to carry
Everything to God in prayer!
O what peace we often forfeit,
O what needless pain we bear!
All because we do not carry
Everything to God in prayer.

Have we trials and temptations?
Is there trouble anywhere?
We should never be discouraged:
Take it to the Lord in prayer.
Can we find a friend so faithful,
Who will all our sorrows share?
Jesus knows our every weakness:
Take it to the Lord in prayer.

Are we weak and heavy-laden,
Cumbered with a load of care?
Precious Saviour, still our refuge:
Take it to the Lord in prayer.
Do thy friends despise, forsake thee?
Take it to the Lord in prayer;
In His arms He'll take and shield thee
Thou wilt find a solace there.

When Scriven wrote the words of this hymn he placed at the top of the page a short text of Scripture, "Pray without ceasing" (1 Thess. 5:17). He then made a copy of the manuscript and sent it to his mother in Ireland. Scriven had never intended that the words should ever be published and no-one else knew of them until the occasion of his own last illness almost thirty years later. At that time Scriven was cared for by a faithful Christian neighbour named James Sackville. They spent much time together and it happened that one night while looking through some of Scriven's papers this neighbour-friend discovered the manuscript of "What a Friend we have in Jesus". He read it through with great delight. "Where did this come from? Who wrote it?" he enquired. "I wrote it" Scriven replied, "The Lord and I did it between us. Many years ago my mother was going through a time of great sorrow and I wrote it to comfort her".

Then, shortly afterwards and under very tragic circumstances, Joseph Scriven departed from this earthly scene of trial and sorrow. His body was laid to rest beside that of his sweetheart Eliza in the little Pengally cemetery near to Bewdley. Some time afterwards there was erected, close to the highway nearby, a large granite monument, a fitting tribute to Scriven's life's work and witness and on it were inscribed the words of his immortal poem: "What a Friend we have in Jesus".

Shortly after Scriven's death the words of his poem appeared in the local newspaper, *The Port Hope Guide*. Some pages from this paper were used for wrapping a parcel which was despatched to New York. The recipient there, on unwrapping the parcel, caught sight of Scriven's poem and thereupon arranged to have it published. Eventually the words came under the notice of the German-American composer, Charles C. Converse, and he set them to music, the simple melody with which they are suitably linked today.

Though over a century has now elapsed since these events, Joseph Scriven still lives on through the lines of his soul-comforting hymn. Its words of help, perhaps most meaningful to those amid life's trials and perplexities, were born out of deep personal experience; they were the fruit of a life mellowed by adversity. In the loneliness of earth's darkest night Scriven had proved the unfailing friendship of the Saviour. He had found in Him a Friend beyond all compare—absolutely faithful, ever loving, deeply interested and fully understanding. Scriven had known besides, only too well, the difficulties and the stresses of life's pathway—its sin, its griefs, its trials, its temptations, its discouragements, its sorrows, its burdens and its disappointments; through them all he had learned to lean hard on the Friend who changes not.

"What a Friend we have in Jesus!"—a Friend who is always available and always approachable. All our concerns matter to Him and He is sufficient for our every need. There is nothing too big for Him and there is nothing too small. His Divine shoulders are strong enough to bear; His Divine heart is tender enough to share, and in His Divine arms we find "a solace there".

"Safe in the arms of Jesus"

Frances Jane Van Alstyne (Fanny Crosby) (1820-1915)

Fanny Crosby.

Among hymn-writers, the name of Fanny Crosby is widely known and greatly loved. Fanny, known affectionately to many in life as "Aunt Fanny" was physically blind; her spiritual vision, however, was unclouded and during her long life-span of ninety-five golden years she composed over eight thousand hymns and poems. Fanny herself has long since passed away to glory; the fragrant memory of her beautiful life and the priceless treasure of her spiritual songs still remain.

Fanny was born in a simple cottage at Southeast, New York, on

March 24th, 1820. Her parents rejoiced greatly at her birth but soon their joy was turned to sorrow for at the age of six weeks, little Fanny's eyes began to inflame. The physician was called but a mistake was made in prescribing treatment and, as the result, Fanny was hopelessly blind for the remainder of life. Fanny, however, was an optimist. She never expressed any word of blame for the physician but in later years was known to say, "It may have been a blunder on the physician's part, but it was no mistake of God's. I verily believe that it was God's intention that I should live my days in physical darkness, so as to be better prepared to sing His praise."

Life for Fanny had its trials; besides, it had its compensations. Her father died ere she had reached her first birthday and thereafter she was cared for by her mother and grandmother. Her blindness deprived her of many of the beautiful things of God's creation; the bright blue sky, the flowers of the field, the golden sunset and the faces of her many dear friends were all hidden from her. However, the devoted attention of mother and grandmother did much to make up for this loss and her grandmother in particular took much time to explain to her the beauties of the world around—of the birds, the flowers, the trees and the wonders of the rainbow.

At the age of fifteen Fanny entered "The Institute for the Blind" in New York and there she spent the next twenty-three years of her life, first as a pupil for twelve years and thereafter as a teacher for a further eleven years. Fanny just loved it. She had a tremendous passion for learning and took a special delight in the works of the great poets and hymn-writers—of Bonar, Montgomery, Longfellow, Tennyson, Wesley, Whittier and of Frances Ridley Havergal in particular; many delightful hours she spent poring over their inspiring compositions.

During this period a remarkable incident happened. Dr. Combe of Boston came one day to the Institute to examine the residents. Placing his hand on Fanny's head and looking into her face he declared, "And here is a poetess; give her every possible encouragement. Read the best books to her, and teach her to appreciate the finest there is in poetry. You will hear from this young lady some day". Dr. Combe's prediction came true and the world, in due course, heard a lot more from Fanny Crosby.

Fanny was converted at the age of thirty. Though, as a child, she had memorised the Holy Scriptures and was able to repeat by heart the five books of Moses, most of the New Testament, many of the Psalms, the Proverbs, the book of Ruth and the Song of Solomon, she did not have that personal knowledge of the Lord Jesus that brings peace to the heart. She longed for it and sought for it and at last she found it. One evening at the close of a meeting, as Dr. Isaac Watts' great hymn, "Alas! and did my Saviour bleed" was being sung, Fanny yielded herself completely to the Saviour for salvation, and that simple faith and assurance of salvation in Christ ever remained precious to her through life.

At the age of thirty-eight Fanny married Alexander Van Alstyne. Alexander was also blind and had come to the Institute eighteen years previously. He was talented and very fond of music. Their mutual interest first drew them together and throughout the forty-four years of their married life, they were very happy and of great help to each other.

Fanny was a great soul and she loved great people—the musicians, the scholars, the preachers, the presidents of her nation. "I wanted to go with the gallant, and sit with the sincere, to associate with those who, like myself, were winning their way, in the face of fiercest foes". She admired and revered the American Presidents who had lived through her own era—Adams, Jackson, Van Buren, Harrison, Tyler, Polk, Clay, Lincoln, Grant, Hayes, Garfield and Cleaveland. Many of them she knew personally; some were her intimate friends and for such men to meet with "the sightless singer" was oft-times for them an inspiration.

Fanny had, besides, a place in her heart for everyone; she found time for ordinary people, she revelled in the company of children. She found much of interest in the lives of others who were handicapped like herself—the works of John Milton, the writings of Helen Keller and the verse of George Matheson were a special joy to her. Her close personal friend, Ira D. Sankey, in the closing years of life lost his sight and these two great souls often found themselves in each others company—weeping together, singing together, praying together or together recounting the many blessings of the Lord. They loved to go back over the years when Sankey had popularised many of Fanny's hymns throughout America and Britain and as the result thousands of souls had been led to Christ for salvation.

The hymns of Fanny Crosby have ever been dearly loved; written originally for the hearts of the people, they readily and rapidly found a place there. Her verse is characterised by a warmth, a tenderness, an intimacy and a simplicity which has scarcely ever been equalled and this is amply evident when we come to such pieces as:

"All the way my Saviour leads me"
"Behold Me standing at the door"
"Blessed assurance, Jesus is mine"
"I am Thine, O Lord"
"Jesus, keep me near the cross"
"Pass me not, O gentle Saviour"
"Praise Him, Praise Him, Jesus our Blessed Redeemer"
"Rescue the perishing"
"Safe in the arms of Jesus"
"Saviour, more than life to me"
"Some day the silver cord will break"
"Thou, my everlasting portion"
"To God be the glory"
"When my life's work is ended"

"Safe in the arms of Jesus" is probably the best known of Fanny's compositions. It was written when she was forty-eight and the circumstances of its writing are of interest—one day her friend, Mr. W. H. Doane came to her: "Fanny," he said, "I have a tune I would like to have you write words for". "Let me hear it," she replied. He played it over and she exclaimed, "That says, 'safe in the arms of Jesus'." She retired to her room and in about thirty minutes returned with the completed hymn:

> Safe in the arms of Jesus,
>   Safe on His gentle breast,
> There by His love o'ershadowed,
>   Sweetly my soul shall rest.
> Hark, 'tis the voice of angels,
>   Borne in a song to me,
> Over the fields of glory,
>   Over the jasper sea.
>
> Safe in the arms of Jesus,
>   Safe from corroding care,
> Safe from the world's temptations,
>   Sin cannot harm me there.
> Free from the blight of sorrow,
>   Free from my doubts and fears,
> Only a few more trials,
>   Only a few more tears.

> *Jesus, my heart's dear refuge,*
>   *Jesus has died for me;*
> *Firm on the Rock of Ages*
>   *Ever my trust shall be.*
> *Here let me wait with patience*
>   *Wait till the night is o'er,*
> *Wait till I see the morning*
>   *Break on the golden shore.*

This simple hymn, with which most of us have been familiar since and love so well, was Fanny's own personal favourite. Its opening words were often upon her lips in life and, in all probability, were the last she spoke before entering the valley of the shadow of death. She passed away at Bridgeport, Connecticut in the early hours of February 12th, 1915, and just before retiring the previous evening she had dictated a letter of sympathy to a bereaved friend; she had concluded it with the words, "know that your precious Ruth is 'safe in the arms of Jesus'."

Some days later Fanny was laid to rest in Bridgeport Cemetery; the occasion was marked by the singing of two of her hymns—"Some day the silver cord will break" and "Safe in the arms of Jesus". Such a choice was most fitting; for "Aunt Fanny" the "some day" of her anticipation had arrived—life's silver cord had been broken and she was "safe in the arms of Jesus".

"The sands of time are sinking"

Anne Ross Cousin (1824-1906)

Anne Ross Cousin.

The writer of this lovely hymn, Mrs. Anne Ross Cousin, was the only daughter of David Ross Cundell of Leith, Scotland. Her father died when she was three and afterwards she with her mother moved to Edinburgh. At the age of twenty-one, Anne married Rev. William Cousin and, thereafter, wholeheartedly identified herself with her husband in his ministry throughout southern Scotland. Mrs. Cousin during her long life composed many hymns and poems. A composite volume of one hundred and seven of these meditations was published in 1876 and entitled, *Immanuel's Land and other pieces by A. R. C.* Two pieces from this collection are still in common usage—one entitled, "The Substitute" ("Oh Christ, what burdens bowed Thy head!") and the other entitled, "Immanuel's Land" ("The sands of time are sinking").

"Immanuel's Land" is the most popular of all Mrs. Cousin's compositions and was written in Irvine about the year 1856 when her husband was minister there. It was first published in 1857 in the *Christian Treasury* and in its original consisted of nineteen verses. Its inspiration and composition stemmed from a long and devoted study by Mrs. Cousin of *The Life and Letters of Samuel Rutherford*. In effect Mrs. Cousin borrowed phrases and imagery from the writings of that notable 17th century Covenanter preacher and wove them skilfully into her composition. The poem or hymn therefore, as we know it today, is the product of these two devoted hearts.

Samuel Rutherford was born in the year 1600 in the Scottish border village of Nisbet and there he spent his early years. Seemingly then he paid scant attention to the needs of his soul and not until he was twenty-seven years of age did he turn to the Saviour. "Like a fool as I was," he said afterwards, "I suffered my sun to be high in the heaven and near afternoon". As a consequence, he ever afterward fervently entreated the young to turn to Christ and give of their best years to Him. In writing to the young man Earlston, he warned, "there is not such a glassy, icy, slippery piece of way betwixt you and Heaven as youth; the devil findeth in youth dry sticks, dry coals and a hot hearth-stone; and how soon he can with his flint cast fire and with his bellows blow it up!". He never wished that any other should imitate him in "loitering on the road too long, and trifling at the gate".

The close of the year 1627 found Rutherford, though only a few months converted to God, as pastor of the rural parish of Anwoth in Galloway. There he ministered for nine years and probably never more diligently did any shepherd labour among his flock than did Samuel Rutherford in Anwoth. Rising at three o'clock in the morning to hold communion with God, he filled each day full for God in diligent study, writing, preaching and visitation. In the pulpit, his delivery was anything but attractive for he had "a strange utterance, a kind of a skreigh" but his messages were alive and warm with the fire of devotion to his Lord. "Many a time I thought he would have flown out of the pulpit when he came to speak of Christ," testified one of his parishioners.

The years at Anwoth were full of trials and often there was little to encourage spiritually. Nevertheless, he never allowed the fire of devotion to Christ to die down in his heart and could not but speak appreciatively of Him to others. Over the unsaved, he yearned most tenderly, "I would lay my dearest joys in the gap between you and eternal destruction . . . I would be glad of one soul . . . My witness is in heaven, your heaven would be two heavens to me and your salvation two salvations . . . " Right to the close of his days, Rutherford held Anwoth fast in his heart:

> *Fair Anwoth by the Solway,*
> *To me thou still art dear!*
> *E'en from the verge of heaven*
> *I drop for thee a tear.*
> *Oh! if one soul from Anwoth*
> *Meet me at God's right hand,*
> *My heaven will be two heavens,*
> *In Immanuel's land.*

The year 1636 brought changes. Sydserff, the new Bishop of Galloway and no lover of Samuel Rutherford, hailed him before the High Commission Court in Wigtown. Rutherford was deposed from office and banished to the distant northern town of Aberdeen. Forbidden to preach, his pen got busy and from that "sea-boat prison" where he and his Lord "held tryst", were despatched letters of the highest spiritual calibre. Some two hundred and twenty of these "prison epistles" have been preserved, *The Letters of Samuel Rutherford*.

Rutherford's exile in Aberdeen ended in 1638 with the signing of the Solemn League and Covenant in which the government recognised the spiritual freedom of the Nonconforming Church. After his liberation Rutherford continued in Scotland as a great spiritual leader and teacher. Settling in St. Andrew's as Professor of Divinity and later as Principal of the new college there, he exercised from that position great influence over students training for the ministry. McWard spoke of St. Andrew's in those days as, "a Lebanon out of which were taken cedars for building the house of the Lord through the whole land". Higher calls to Edinburgh the Scottish capital, and to Utrecht and Harderwyck in Holland were declined, for Rutherford felt convinced that God's will for him was at St. Andrew's and there he remained.

The year 1660 was marked by the death of Cromwell and the ascendancy of King Charles II. Dark storm clouds gathered. In the following year, Rutherford was deposed from all his offices at St. Andrew's and summoned by the Duke of Middleton to answer to Parliament on a charge of high treason. When the summons reached Rutherford at St. Andrew's he was on his death-bed, but to the messengers he gave a prompt and clear reply, "Tell them," he said, "that I have a summons already from a superior Judge and judicatory, and I behove to answer my first summons and, ere your day arrive, I will be where few kings and great folks come". When Rutherford's reply was received by the Council, their wrath waxed hot and with feeble malice they resolved that he must not be allowed to die within the college walls. Nevertheless, in the Council that day one voice was heard in Rutherford's defence. Lord Burleigh stood alone and declared, "ye have voted that honest man out of his college but ye cannot vote him out of Heaven".

> *They've summoned me before them,*
> *But there I may not come—*
> *My Lord says, "Come up hither",*
> *My Lord says, "Welcome Home!"*
> *My kingly King, at His white throne,*
> *My presence doth command,*
> *Where glory—glory dwelleth*
> *In Immanuel's Land.*

Within a few days Rutherford had answered his first summons into the presence of his Lord, the righteous Judge, and away from all the "wranglings and cruelty of wicked men".

Rutherford, like Paul the apostle, was a man of singular affection and purpose. His heart's contemplation was Christ. "That is Rutherford's glory, his absorption in Christ" is the testimony of Alexander Smellie, "he has but one goal and no other is worth the mentioning". Dr. Taylor Innes describes him as a man, "impatient on earth, intolerant of sin, rapt into the continual contemplation of one unseen Face". In that contemplation through the Scriptures, Rutherford discovered lovely figures of Christ's person and in each one he perceived a unique glory—the fragrance of the Rose—the beauty of the King—the glory of the Lamb—the supply of the Fountain—the reliability of the Guide—the virtue of the Bridegroom and the grace of the Beloved One. Even in these, he acknowledged there were limitations, for he confessed that, "no pen, no words, no image can express to you the loveliness of my only, only Lord Jesus".

Rutherford, as did John the beloved disciple, reclined upon the bosom of the Eternal. In his letters he would exhort others to do the same, "There are many heads lying in Christ's bosom, and there is room for yours among the rest... Go where ye will, your souls shall not sleep sound but in Christ's bosom"—and from that place of sacred intimacy, he went forth to declare Him to others. A fitting testimony to the man and his message has been borne by the 17th century London merchant who, on returning home, announced that he brought great news—he had been converted. "I came," he said, "I came to Irvine and heard a well-favoured proper old man with a long beard, David Dickson by name, and that man showed me all my heart. Then I went to St. Andrew's where I heard a sweet majestic-looking man, Robert Blair by name, and he showed me the majesty of God. After him I heard a little fair man and he showed me the loveliness of Christ"; and that "little fair man" was Samuel Rutherford.

The direction of Rutherford's heart was "into the love of God, and into the patient waiting for Christ" (II Thess. 3:5). He mourned his own soul's limited capacity while down here on earth. "I am only pained that He hath such beauty and fairness... and I bleared eyes". Sharing the passion of Adoniram Judson who exclaimed, "Oh, the love of Christ... we cannot comprehend it now, but what a study in eternity!", Rutherford too longed for that moment when the last sands of time would have run through life's glass and then would dawn the day of unclouded vision and unlimited appreciation:

> The sands of time are sinking,
>   The dawn of heaven breaks.
> The summer morn I've sighed for,
>   The fair sweet morn awakes:
> Dark, dark hath been the midnight,
>   But dayspring is at hand,
> And glory—glory dwelleth
>   In Immanuel's land.

Oh Christ! He is the Fountain,
  The deep sweet well of love;
The streams on earth I've tasted,
  More deep I'll drink above:
There to an ocean fulness
  His mercy doth expand,
And glory—glory dwelleth
  In Immanuel's land.

"There's a Friend for little children"

Albert Midlane (1825-1909)

Albert Midlane.

The Isle of Wight has been the home of many hymn-writers. Thomas Ken, author of "Praise God, from whom all blessings flow" spent two years in the village of Brighstone. Alfred Tennyson, author of, "Strong Son of God, immortal Love" had his home at Farringford, Freshwater. Samuel Trevor Francis, author of "O the deep, deep love of Jesus" lived for a few years at Ryde. Jemima Luke, author of "I think, when I read the sweet story of old" and Mary Fowler Maude, author of "Thine for ever! God of Love", both lived their later years and died at an advanced age in the town of Newport. Thomas Binney wrote "Eternal Light, Eternal Light!" during his five year pastorate in the Congregational Church of Newport and Albert Midlane, author of many well-known gospel and children's hymns lived a long lifetime in that same town and has left there many lasting and fragrant memories.

Of these seven hymn-writers, Albert Midlane was the only one born on the Isle, the only true "Islander". He was the youngest child of James and Fanny Midlane of Carisbrooke Parish, Isle of Wight and was born January 23rd, 1825, three months after the death of his father. He had a deeply spiritual mother and a godly devoted sister. He recalls "how often from the cares of the family would the dear mother lead me into a quiet room; and there kneeling by my side would she, with holy fervour, by prayer bring God into all her circumstances down here; or by sweet communion be with God above them all". Thus, "there came at an early period, into the mind of one enjoying such holy influences, clear convictions concerning his state before God". He experienced the blessing of salvation at a Sunday-school Teachers' Prayer Meeting and soon afterwards was baptized at Castlehold Baptist Church in Newport. At the age of twenty-three and after exercise before the Lord, he dissociated himself from the Baptist Church and met with like-minded believers in assembly fellowship.

In early life, Albert Midlane served three years in the printer's trade and then entered the hardware business. As an ironmonger and tin smith by trade, he progressed to establish his own business in Newport. His kindness and generosity toward all was almost unlimited and as a consequence he experienced financial difficulty toward the close of his business career; however, such was his Christian testimony that loyal friends rallied to his relief, and as the result of their liberality Midlane, in the declining years of life, was left with an annuity. As an employer, he was very highly respected by his staff and some served in his employment for fifty years.

Albert Midlane's chief interests, however, were in the things of the Lord. He gave much of his time to Sunday-school work, to the preaching of the gospel, both indoor and in the open air, and to the teaching of the Word of God. From early life right to its close, he gave himself unsparingly to these things and just three months before he died we find him, as an old man of eighty-four, standing in the open air in Newport addressing a large crowd of his fellow townsfolk and speaking to them of things eternal.

Albert Midlane was talented as a hymn-writer. In his early poetical efforts, he was encouraged first by his Sunday-school teacher and then by Thomas Binney who lived nearby. He published hymns and poems throughout life, his first appearing at the age of seventeen and his last in commemoration of his eighty-fourth birthday. The old castle at Carisbrooke was his favourite retreat for meditation and there many of his best hymns were born. "Most of my hymns have been written during walks round the historical ancient ruins of Carisbrooke Castle. The twilight hour, so dear to thought, and the hushed serenity then pervading nature, had often allured my soul to deep and uninterrupted meditation which, in its turn, has given birth to lines which, had not these walks been taken, would never have been penned".

Albert Midlane's hymns and poems number about one thousand and many are still in use today. A large number of the soul-stirring gospel hymns sung nightly throughout our land have come from his pen:

> "A sweet remembrance fills my soul"
> "All things are ready,—Come!"
> "Calvary's Cross is, to the sinner"
> "Can you count me the leaves of the forest tree?"
> "Hark, the voice of Jesus calling"
> "Himself He could not save"
> "How blest are the scriptures, they tell us of love"
> "How solemn are the words"
> "I once was bound in Satan's chains"
> "Jesus lived. He lived for sinners"
> "Not all the gold of all the world"
> "Oh wondrous grace! that found a plan"
> "Oh, what a glorious truth is this—Jesus died"
> "Oh, what a Saviour is Jesus the Lord!"
> "Passing onward, quickly passing"
> "Perfect salvation—Jesus has died"
> "Redeemed! how the scriptures proclaim it"
> "Salvation! oh salvation! endearing, precious sound"
> "Salvation, what a precious sound"
> "When the Saviour said, 'Tis finished'"

The content of gospel truth in such a collection is very varied—in some are words of warning, in others words of appeal; some are words of salvation and others express assurance and peace. Of his compositions, Mr. Josiah Miller has stated that, "Mr. Midlane's hymns are full of spiritual thought, careful in their wording and often very pleasing without reaching the highest form of practical excellence". Dr. John Julian says, "a marked feature of these hymns is the constant and happy use of Scripture phraseology"—indeed throughout, Midlane is loyal to the Word of God. Two volumes of Midlane's gospel hymns were compiled and published during his lifetime—*Gospel Echoes* in 1865 and *The Gospel Hall Hymn Book* when the author was in his eightieth year. Midlane has also given to us two other favourite hymns—his lovely devotional hymn, "Lord, when I think upon the love" and his soul-stirring revival hymn, "Revive Thy work, O Lord".

However, it is as a writer of hymns for children that Albert Midlane is renowned. He loved children and loved to hear them sing. In his own experience, it had been a godly Sunday-school teacher that had helped to shape his early life and had prompted his first poetic efforts. It was at a Sunday-school Teachers' Prayer Meeting that he personally found the Saviour. A children's hymn, "God Bless Our Sunday-school" was the first of his compositions to receive publicity. As a consequence, Sunday-school work was to have a large place in Midlane's heart and life. He wrote many hymns for children and *The Bright Blue Sky Hymn Book*, first published in 1867, contained many of these. His "A little lamb went straying" is widely known and much loved but it is his "There's a Friend for little children" that has received almost universal acclaim and holds a special place in nearly all our hearts.

> There's a Friend for little children
>   Above the bright blue sky,
> A Friend Who never changes,
>   Whose love will never die;
> Our earthly friends may fail us,
>   And change with changing years,
> This Friend is always worthy
>   Of that dear Name He bears.

There's a home for little children
  Above the bright blue sky,
Where Jesus reigns in glory,
  A home of peace and joy;
No home on earth is like it,
  Nor can with it compare;
For every one is happy,
  Nor could be happier there.

There's a song for little children
  Above the bright blue sky,
A song that will not weary,
  Though sung continually;
A song which even angels
  Can never, never sing;
They know not Christ as Saviour,
  But worship Him as King.

Three further verses tell of "a rest for little children", "a crown for little children" and "a robe for little children".

This delightful children's hymn of Midlane's was written on the night of February 27th, 1859 and the record of its composition is as follows: "Stimulated by a passionate desire to write something special for the little ones, Mr. Midlane, after a busy business day, settled down in the quiet of the evening to what proved the great task of his life, and by 2 o'clock in the morning his supreme effort in hymnology was completed ... ". He entitled it, "Above the bright blue sky" and it was first published as a closing article in the December issue, 1859, of C. Mackintosh's children's magazine, *Good News for the Little Ones.*

Its popular tune, "In Memoriam" was composed in 1875 by Sir John Stainer in memory of his little boy, Frederick Henry Stainer, who had died but a few months previously.

Albert Midlane lived to see the impact of the first fifty years of this hymn. It found its way into hundreds of hymn books and to all five continents of the world. It was translated into some fifty languages. At its jubilee, in the early part of 1909, Mr. Midlane had the great pleasure of hearing it sung by three thousand children in St. Paul's Cathedral, London, and again by hundreds of children in his own home-town of Newport, as from the Victoria Monument he surveyed the large sea of little faces assembled in the open market square to pay their tribute. Nor did its singing cease when Albert Midlane, its composer, passed away at day-break, Lord's Day, February, 27th 1909, for as his body was laid to rest in Carisbrooke Cemetery, March 4th, 1909, its strains once more filled the air and rose to Heaven from a company of children standing around the open grave. Ere its music had died away the interment of a child in a grave nearby added to the pathos of the scene. The grave of Albert Midlane is marked today by a memorial stone subscribed for by the Sunday-school children of Hampshire and the Isle of Wight.

Albert Midlane through life was a friend of little children. He loved them, served them and gave to them a song. His deep desire and prayer for them, however, was this—that early in life they might come to know the Saviour and enjoy in Heaven for ever the society of an unchangeable Friend, the shelter of an imperishable home and the sweetness of an unwearying song.

"Peace, perfect peace"

Edward Henry Bickersteth (1825-1906)

Edward Henry Bickersteth.

Edward Henry Bickersteth was born January 1825, at Islington and was named after his father and grandfather. His grandfather, Henry Bickersteth, had been a surgeon in Kirkby-Lonsdale, Westmoreland. His father, Edward Bickersteth, was a minister in the Church of England, a godly man who, after spending much of his life in the service of the Church Missionary Society, gave the last twenty years of his ministry to the parishioners of Watton, Hertfordshire.

Edward Henry grew up at Watton Rectory. His childhood there

was packed with activity and was unforgettable. The "Recollections" of his sister, Emily, permit a look-in on life at the Rectory in those days, "At 5.30 every morning an alarm clock went off and aroused Edward who tumbled half asleep into a shower-bath and soon roused all his sisters by vigorous knocks on their doors. In an hour's time, all were downstairs, the boys at work with their tutor...The rector himself spent part of this time in a retired walk, engaged in his devotions. At 7.50 he returned from his walk and gathered his children into his study where each one repeated passages of the Holy Scriptures of their own choosing, some of them learning whole books of the Bible".

During his days at Watton Rectory, Edward got to know the Saviour. On a Sunday afternoon, after months of spiritual hunger and struggle and while reading Krummacher's *Elijah the Tishbite*, he committed himself to the Saviour for salvation and entered into the peace and joy of knowing that he belonged to Christ. He was then fourteen years of age and soon afterwards dedicated his life to the service of God.

Edward entered Trinity College, Cambridge, when he was eighteen and after four years of diligent study graduated B.A. with honours in 1847. He gained his M.A. three years later. After ordination in the Church of England he held two short curacies from 1848-1852, at Banningham in Norfolk and at Tunbridge Wells in Kent. Then after three years as rector of Hinton-Martell in Dorset, he was appointed to Christ Church, Hampstead.

At Hampstead, Bickersteth entered upon his labours with enthusiasm and with diligence. The work was large and his days were busy. Nevertheless he found time for those things which lay close to his heart. The preaching of the gospel occupied much of his time. He personally proclaimed its glorious message both indoors and in the open air and took a great interest in its progress in foreign lands. It was, indeed, a great joy to him when two of his sons gave themselves to overseas missionary service, one to India and the other to Japan. Thus busily, devotedly and faithfully, Bickersteth ministered to the people of Hampstead for thirty years and those years were fruitful for God.

In 1885, Bickersteth was appointed Bishop of Exeter and in that office he continued with all his wonted enthusiasm and diligence for fifteen years till ill health overtook him. This forced his resignation and he then moved to London. For over five years he suffered bodily weakness; nevertheless, through it all, his faith remained strong and on May 16th, 1906 he passed away from "earth's struggles" to "heaven's perfect peace".

E. H. Bickersteth was endowed with a fine poetic gift and throughout life devoted much of his time to the furtherance of hymnology. As a compiler his best work was his *Hymnal Companion*, first published in 1870. As a composer, Bickersteth ranks among the finest of his day. His subject matter was diverse—some of his hymns were gospel, some missionary but most were written for the encouragement and comfort of the people of God. The features of his compositions have received fitting comment by Dr. John Julian " . . . there is a smooth plaintiveness and individuality in his hymns which give them a distinct character of their own. His thoughts are usually with the individual, and not with the mass; with the single soul and his God and not with a vast multitude bowed in adoration before the Almighty. Hence, although many of his hymns are eminently suited to congregational purposes, and have attained to a wide popularity, yet his finest productions are those which are best suited for private use".

The best known of Bickersteth's hymns is "Peace, perfect peace". Though often sung by collected companies of God's people, it is a fine example of a hymn suited for private use; in this capacity it was a great favourite with Queen Victoria.

This lovely hymn was written by Bickersteth in August, 1875, during the period of his Hampstead ministry. At that time, the Bickersteths, as a family, had gone on holiday to Harrogate in Yorkshire. For some years the usual practice of the family at Sunday tea-time had been for each member to quote a hymn of their choosing and for father to conclude the session with one of his choice or of his own making. In the morning of the Sunday in question, Bickersteth had been to hear the vicar of Harrogate preach from the lovely text of Isaiah 26:3, "Thou wilt keep him in perfect peace, whose mind is stayed on Thee." In the afternoon he went for a solitary walk on the moors. The beauty of the phrase, "perfect peace" filled and flooded his mind. He then called on a sick relative and found him bravely fighting a terminal illness but ill at ease spiritually. Bickersteth's afternoon's meditation, "perfect peace", then took shape in verse and the sharing of it brought great comfort to his dying friend. Later that same afternoon at the tea-table he read to his family the lines of his completed hymn:

Peace, perfect peace, in this dark world of sin?
The blood of Jesus whispers peace within.

Peace, perfect peace, by thronging duties pressed?
To do the will of Jesus, this is rest.

Peace, perfect peace, with sorrows surging round?
On Jesus' bosom naught but calm is found.

Peace, perfect peace, with loved ones far away?
In Jesus' keeping we are safe, and they.

Peace, perfect peace, our future all unkown?
Jesus we know and He is on the throne.

Peace, perfect peace, death shadowing us and ours?
Jesus hath vanquished death and all its powers.

It is enough: earth's struggles soon shall cease
And Jesus call us to heaven's perfect peace.

"Perfect peace" is the English rendering of the beautiful Hebrew, "Shalom Shalom" of Isaiah 26:3 and bespeaks the inner tranquility of the human heart stayed upon and kept by Jehovah. That uninterrupted blessedness was the portion on earth of the Lord Jesus, amid the vicissitudes of life. In a world of sin, away from home, amid earth's sorrows, subject to life's pressures, and even when overshadowed by death, His heart enjoyed its perfect rest. He called it, "My peace" and, as a precious legacy, bequeathed it to His own (John 14:27).

This inner peace of the believer is daily assailed and threatened. Bickersteth in his hymn, however, assures us that for each distressing perplexity that comes our way, there is a corresponding Divine supply. The opening six stanzas, each in the form of question and answer, speak of:

A peace amid earth's defilement through Jesus precious blood,
A rest amid earth's pressure in Jesus perfect will,
A repose amid earth's struggles on Jesus priestly bosom,
A serenity amid earth's separations through Jesus present keeping,
An assurance amid earth's apprehensions in Jesus perpetual control,
A cheer amid earth's gloom because of Jesus personal victory.

The closing stanza points onward beyond this world to "heaven's perfect peace". The things that vex us now will then be no more—"no more curse" to blight that heavenly place, "no more death" to cast its long dark shadow, "no more sorrow" to crush the tender and broken spirit and "no more sea" to ever again cause another separation. The former things will have passed away; then God and the Lamb will reign supreme and every heart will know its "perfect peace".

"Throned upon the awful Tree"

John Ellerton (1826-1893)

John Ellerton.

In the world of hymnology, the name of John Ellerton is both familiar and famous. As a hymn-writer, his hymns are immortal. As a compiler, he brought order out of chaos. As a translator, he recovered much hidden treasure. As an adviser, his counsel was widely sought and highly esteemed, and as an illustrator, his contribution was enormous. John Ellerton was first of all a minister of Christ and afterwards a poet. He first fulfilled the solemn charge committed to him, "Preach the Word; be instant in season and out of

211

season; reprove, rebuke, exhort with all longsuffering and doctrine'' (II Tim. 4:2), but thereafter he used whatever time he had to hand in the furtherance of hymnology. Throughout life, hymns were his joy and delight. In death, he passed away with the words of hymns upon his lips. He was laid to rest, ''among his own hymns'' and today is best remembered as an hymnologist with few equals whose consecrated gift was entirely for the honour of his Lord.

John Ellerton was born in the city of London on December 16th, 1826. His parents, George and Jemima Frances Ellerton, had come from a strongly evangelical Yorkshire family. Theirs was a simple faith in God, and the Ellerton home, though devoid of many of the luxuries of life, was characterized by simplicity and happiness. John's father was a good-humoured and kindly man. His mother was a deeply spiritual woman and the guide of his early youth.

At eighteen, John entered Trinity College, Cambridge, and followed there a brilliant literary career. In those days he had opportunity to exercise his naturally-endowed poetic gift, and of his many compositions the most outstanding was his English poem, ''The Death of Baldur'' which he submitted for the Chancellor's prize.

After graduation, Ellerton entered the Church of England and for over forty years ministered faithfully to the congregations of some six parishes scattered throughout his homeland. First he held curacies at Easebourne in Sussex and at St. Nicholas in Brighton and during this ten years period, gave himself unreservedly to the service of God and of others. Though the days were busy, he found time for study and the pursuit of his poetic gift and while at Brighton he composed a number of hymns, mainly for children, and compiled a small children's hymnal, *Hymns for Schools and Bible Classes* (1859).

In 1860 John married Charlotte Alicia Hart from Brighton and the first twelve years of their wedded life were spent at Crewe Green in Cheshire. There, as minister to the villagers and as domestic chaplain to Lord Crewe, John laboured energetically and sacrificially. This period was to mark the beginning of his fame, both as a composer and as a translator of hymns and, in a brief space of two years, he wrote some twenty-six hymns of the first rank. From Crewe Green, Ellerton moved to the seclusion of a quiet rural parish at Hinstock in Shropshire and it was here that his best work on hymns was done but with a change of emphasis. From being a composer, he now devoted more and more time to the compiling and the illustration of hymns.

This tremendous task of detailing the authorship and history of hundreds of hymns occupied much of his time. The work, however, he found both pleasant and interesting.

The years 1876-84 were spent in a busy ministry at Barnes in Surrey near to London. By this time his expertise in the whole field of hymnology was widely recognised and heavy demands were made almost daily upon his time and talent. Under the strain, his health broke down and in the spring of 1884, he was forced to resign his charge. However, several months in the less-demanding and restful centres of Veytoux in Switzerland and Pegli in Italy effected restoration of health and in the following year (1885), Ellerton returned to England to White Roding in Essex and there he remained till the onset of his last illness at the age of sixty-five. He, thereupon, retired to Torquay but suffered a further deterioration in health some months later and died on June 15th, 1893. His burial at Torquay was marked by the singing of some six of his own hymns.

John Ellerton was a scholar who had few equals. Professor Henry Atwell wrote of him as, "a man of deep learning" and described "that rare and indefinable something which radiates from poetic natures, and makes other hearts burn within them". He was noted for his tender sympathy and his intense lovingness. By nature he was a shy and sensitive man and yet the truest and tenderest of friends. His associates affectionately spoke of him as, "dear Ellerton".

As a hymn-writer, John Ellerton has left for succeeding generations a very large and rich legacy. Ellerton's own estimate of his work, however, was both self-effacing and Christ-exalting. "If counted worthy to contribute to Christ's praise in the congregation, one ought to feel thankful and very humble". No less than eighty-six hymns proceeded from his pen and some seventy-six of these were compiled and published in 1888 as his, *Hymns, Original and Translated*. Honesty, simplicity and reverence were the hallmarks of all his compositions. Henry Housman, his biographer, says, "No writer was ever more careful not to put into the lips of a congregation, words which, as Christians, they could not make their own."

Ellerton's best-loved hymns are specially suited for congregational singing and many are appropriate to special times or occasions. "Saviour, again to Thy dear Name we raise" is an evening hymn. It was written in 1866 and it ranked among the finest of his compositions. "Now the labourer's task is o'er" is a funeral hymn and was penned in 1871. "The day Thou gavest, Lord, is ended" was first composed as a missionary hymn but later adopted as an evening hymn. Queen Victoria made choice of this hymn to be sung throughout the land on the occasion of her Diamond Jubilee in 1897. Ellerton's wedding hymn, "O Father, all-creating" was written in 1876 at the request of the Duke of Westminster for the occasion of the marriage of his daughter. "Throned upon the Awful Tree" was written in 1875 at the request of Sir Henry Williams Baker for his new edition of *Hymns, Ancient and Modern*. When published it was entitled "Good Friday". Of Ellerton's hymns, it has been judged by Dr. John Julian as "the grandest of all his original compositions":

> *Throned upon the awful Tree,*
> *King of grief, I watch with Thee;*
> *Darkness veils Thine anguished face,*
> *None its lines of woe can trace,*
> *None can tell what pangs unknown*
> *Hold Thee silent and alone.*
>
> *Silent through those three dread hours,*
> *Wrestling with the evil powers;*
> *Left alone with human sin,*
> *Gloom around Thee and within,*
> *Till the appointed time is nigh,*
> *Till the Lamb of God may die.*
>
> *Hark that cry that peals aloud*
> *Upward through the whelming cloud!*
> *Thou, the Father's only Son,*
> *Thou, His own Anointed One,*
> *Thou dost ask Him—can it be:*
> *Why hast Thou forsaken Me?*

This impressive crucifixion hymn speaks of the experience and anguish of the Lord Jesus on Calvary. The waters truly are deep. Ellerton seeks to penetrate beyond their storm-tossed surface to reach the hidden billows underneath—"The Father's only Son", "His own anointed One,"—left alone with human sin in an impenetrable darkness! Forsaken! . . . For us a light is shed in a fourth verse, added by Ellerton at a later date, declaring that because of

Calvary, no trusting soul need ever experience the abandonment of God even in its most dark and appalling night,

> Lord, should fear and anguish roll
> Darkly o'er my sinful soul,
> Thou, who once was thus bereft
> That Thine own might ne'er be left,
> Teach me by that bitter cry
> In the gloom to know Thee nigh.

"When peace, like a river"

Horatio Gates Spafford (1828-1888)

Horatio G. Spafford.

Horatio G. Spafford wrote this hymn in the midst of a very dark experience. He was a well-to-do Christian lawyer from the city of Chicago who had, but a short time previously, lost his only son; soon after that the great fire of Chicago swept away his heavy investments on the shores of Lake Michigan. He then decided to have a break and planned a European tour for himself, his wife and their four daughters. This was in the fall of 1873.

Last minute business matters, however, detained Mr. Spafford from accompanying his wife and girls to Europe on board the French steamer, the *Ville de Havre*; but he intended to follow them a few days later. The *Ville de Havre*, the largest ship afloat at that time, was about two-thirds of its way across the Atlantic when, at two o'clock in the morning of November 22nd, 1873, it collided with an English sailing vessel, The *Lochearn*. The *Ville de Havre* foundered rapidly, going down inside half an hour, but before it did so Mrs. Spafford knelt in prayer with her four children asking God that they might be saved or made ready to die, whichever was His will. The four children perished but Mrs. Spafford was among the twenty-eight survivors picked up by another ship and landed nine days later at Cardiff. She immediately cabled her husband, **"SAVED ALONE"**, a meaningful message which he later had framed and hung in his office.

Mr. Spafford then took the first available boat to join his bereaved wife in England; in deep heart sorrow he crossed the Atlantic. It is reported that on board the vessel, and when near to the spot of the children's watery grave, he penned the words of this immortal hymn:

> *When peace, like a river, attendeth my way,*
> *When sorrows, like sea-billows, roll;*
> *Whatever my lot, Thou hast taught me to know*
> *It is well, it is well with my soul.*
>
> *It is well with my soul,*
> *It is well, it is well with my soul.*
>
> *Though Satan should buffet, though trials should come,*
> *Let this blest assurance control,*
> *That Christ hath regarded my helpless estate,*
> *And hath shed His own blood for my soul.*
>
> *My sin—oh, the bliss of this glorious thought—*
> *My sin—not in part, but the whole,*
> *Is nailed to His cross; and I bear it no more;*
> *Praise the Lord, praise the Lord, O my soul!*
>
> *For me, be it Christ, be it Christ hence to live;*
> *If Jordan above me should roll*
> *No pang shall be mine, for in death as in life,*
> *Thou wilt whisper Thy peace to my soul.*

But Lord, 'tis for Thee, for Thy coming, we wait,
  The sky, not the grave is our goal;
Oh, trump of the angel! Oh, voice of the Lord!
  Blessèd hope! blessèd rest of my soul!

At that time, D. L. Moody and Ira D. Sankey well-known friends of the Spafford family were holding meetings in the city of Edinburgh. When they received the tragic news they made their way south to meet with the sorrowing parents and try to offer them some comfort. Much to their surprise, however, they found Mr. and Mrs. Spafford completely at peace, sustained by God and able to say, "It is well, God's will be done".

Some months later, back in the Spafford home in the city of Chicago, Mr. Sankey discovered the verses of Horatio's composition and on reading them exclaimed, "These words are inspired. It is a hymn that millions will be singing for their inspiration and comfort".

God later gave to the Spaffords three other children—a boy who died when three years old and two girls, Bertha and Grace. In 1881, Mr. and Mrs. Spafford, together with the two girls, moved to the city of Jerusalem and there with the help of some Christian friends set up the American Colony for the care of the sick and destitute. One of the first boys they received into the colony was Jacob Eliahu, a twelve year-old Spanish Jew. Jacob was an orphan but some time later he was adopted into the Spafford home and given the name of Jacob Spafford.

Jacob, two years prior to his coming to the Spafford home, had made a very interesting discovery in the Old City of Jerusalem. One day, as he was playing with another boy at the pool of Siloam, they ventured to go into the dark tunnel through which the water entered the pool. As they advanced further and further along the dark underground channel, they were suddenly startled by the noise of gushing water. Thus frightened, they hurriedly turned back and made for the entrance but, in so doing, Jacob slipped and, while trying to regain his poise, discovered with the palm of his outstretched hand an inscribed stone slab in the wall of the underground channel. This stone, the now-famous Siloam inscription, told of the excavation of the underground water channel by King Hezekiah in 700 B.C.; it is the oldest piece of Hebrew writing known today.

In the year 700 B.C., the city of Jerusalem was about to be besieged by King Sennacherib, the ruthless Assyrian. The only water supply to the city, the Gihon spring, was accessible only from outside the city wall. In order to hide the waters of the Gihon spring from the approaching enemy and bring them inside the besieged city, King Hezekiah engineered an underground water channel. His quarry men worked with all haste from both ends, hewing their way through the solid rock until they met; the water then flowed inside the city and the outer spring was sealed off from the enemy. The fascinating account of the hewing of Hezekiah's underground water channel and in particular of the dramatic meeting of the quarry men working from both ends was recorded in detail on the Siloam inscription stone found some two thousand five hundred years later by our young friend Jacob Eliahu.

Jacob's interesting discovery in the year 1880 speaks to us of a city under siege. Without, the enemy was battering at her gates and pouring scorn and taunts upon her inhabitants, yet within all was well. In like manner, H. G. Spafford (Jacob's father by adoption), in his hymn, pictures the soul of the believer under siege. Though the storm be ever so fierce and the assault of the enemy ever so furious, yet within, all is well. There faith sits serene and calm, the contemplation of Calvary's full redemption and its glorious consummation at the Rapture enabling her to sing, "It is well, it is well with my soul".

"There were ninety and nine"

Elizabeth Cecilia Douglas Clephane (1830-1869)

Bridgend House, Melrose.
(Where Eliz. C. Clephane wrote "The ninety and nine").

One afternoon in May, 1874, two American evangelists, Dwight L. Moody and Ira D. Sankey boarded a train in Glasgow. They were on their way to Edinburgh to commence their second mission in the Scottish capital. On the platform in Glasgow, Mr. Sankey had bought a newspaper and during the journey he looked through it in the hope of finding some items of interest, maybe some American news. Just before reaching his destination his eye caught some lines written in an unobtrusive corner of one of its pages:

There were ninety and nine that safely lay
  In the shelter of the fold,
But one was out on the hills away,
  Far off from the gates of gold—
Away on the mountains wild and bare,
Away from the tender Shepherd's care.

"Lord, Thou hast here Thy ninety and nine;
  Are they not enough for Thee?"
But the Shepherd made answer, "This of Mine
  Has wandered away from Me:
And although the road be rough and steep,
I go to the desert to find My sheep".

He read the lines over to his companion. Mr. Moody, however, was so engrossed in writing a letter that he scarcely heard. Sankey cut the verses out of the paper and placed them in his music scrap book.

On the second day, that never-to-be-forgotten noonday meeting of the mission in Edinburgh, Mr. Moody spoke with all his wonted fervour on the parable of the lost sheep from Luke 15. Dr. Andrew Bonar then got up to address the audience. Mr. Moody whispered to Mr. Sankey sitting by his side on the platform, requesting him to sing some appropriate solo at the close of the meeting. But what should he sing? Suddenly the thought flashed into his mind, "Sing the words you read in the train". But he had no music. His heart went up to God, for he felt that he must sing those words. He sat down to the organ and the music came note by note, based on an old plantation melody, "A wonderful stream is the river of time", which he had once heard in the Southern States of America. He was helped of God to complete the first verse, then the second, the third and right through all the hymn. What a close that was to the meeting! Hearts were touched and moved by the love of Christ and many lost ones were found by the Shepherd. This remarkable story tells of the first occasion when this hymn, "The ninety and nine" was sung in public and wedded to the lovely tune with which we are so familiar today.

Some years afterwards, a young Englishman from a lovely Christian home found himself in a hotel in Paris. He had gone there to enjoy himself and to get away from the influence of home. In the hotel he found lying on the reading table an English copy of Mr. Sankey's hymns. He had heard of Sankey. His sister, Mary, used to speak often of Moody and Sankey and had tried to influence him to attend their meetings, but he had resented it. Nevertheless, curiosity caused him to flick over the pages and he was arrested by words which caught his eye, "But one was out on the hills away, far off from the gates of gold". "Perhaps, Mary would say that about me!" he thought. He closed the book and went off to the opera, but he could not enjoy it. Those words kept repeating themselves in his mind. He came back to the hotel, found the book again and read through the whole hymn. God was speaking to his heart. Now he knew and felt within that he was the one "far off from the gates of gold". God used the words of that lovely hymn, portraying the love of Christ for sinners, as the means of his salvation.

The words of "the ninety and nine" were written by Elizabeth Cecilia Douglas Clephane, the third and youngest daughter of Andrew Douglas Clephane of Carlogie, the Sheriff-Principal of Fife and Kinross and a descendant of an old and honourable Scottish family. Elizabeth was born in Edinburgh on June 10th, 1830. When she was eight years of age her father died. The family then moved to Ormiston but at the time of the writing of the hymn, Elizabeth was living with her two unmarried sisters (her mother having also died) at Bridgend House near to Melrose in Roxburghshire.

Elizabeth was by nature a talented girl, though of a quiet and retiring disposition. Her biographer tells of her, "While still young in years she learned the meaning of sorrow through the death of both her parents, but this experience of bereavement, together with a weak physical frame which characterised her all her days, far from embittering her, added a sweetness and charm to her gentle spirit, and equipped her for that tender and gracious ministry of helpfulness which won for her from the poor and suffering of Melrose the name of 'The Sunbeam'."

Elizabeth had three brothers. The eldest, named George, left home at the age of twenty three and went to Canada. There he fell in with bad company and, as the result, became a partner in their vices. Then one morning, some nine years later, he was picked up from the roadside and carried to the home of a Dr. Mutch; there he died. When the tragic news reached the three sisters in Melrose, Elizabeth, who was then about twenty-one years of age, was deeply affected. She retired to her room and closed the door. Her heart was breaking and she wanted to give expression to her feelings. "George had wandered from the fold! Had he been, however, beyond the reach of the

Shepherd?" So, taking pen and paper, she set down in verse the words of "the ninety and nine" and when finished, she took the manuscript and locked it away in her desk, not wishing for anyone else to see it.

Then some seventeen years later the words appeared in print in *The Children's Hour* (1868); whether the manuscript had lain in her desk for all that time, or whether it had been lost and the hymn rewritten, is difficult to ascertain. Elizabeth died on February 19th in the following year (1869) and shortly after her death, the words of "the ninety and nine" together with some other of her works in verse received wider publication in *The Family Treasury* under the title-heading, "Breathings from the Border".

This hymn, "the ninety and nine" may be described as immortal. Mrs. E. R. Pitman in her book on lady hymn-writers states, "Miss Clephane, by this hymn, has set in motion a sermon on the love of Christ which will never die as long as the English tongue is spoken. Only in the last great day will it be known how many wandering sheep have been brought to Jesus by its means. It is like most of the hymns that come from the heart of woman—tender, touching and true".

The Scripture on which the hymn is based is the parable of the lost sheep told by the Saviour almost two thousand years ago—a sheep was lost and it mattered much to the shepherd: he counted no expense too great and no distance too far if only he might find it again and bring it back home. The graphic earthly story is then outstripped by the heavenly for, like the sheep, the sinner was lost, away from the Shepherd. Then the Shepherd left the glory to seek the lost. The distance He had to go was immeasurable, the difficulties encountered, the darkness and the deep beyond computation. Notwithstanding, love took Him all the way; He found the lost and secured it again at infinite cost. Joy unbounded filled His heart, then reverberated through realms celestial:

> *But none of the ransomed ever knew*
> *How deep were the waters crossed;*
> *Nor how dark was the night that the Lord passed through*
> *Ere He found His sheep that was lost.*
> *Out in the desert He heard its cry—*
> *Sick and helpless, and ready to die.*

"Lord, whence are those blood-drops all the way
 That mark out the mountain's track?"
"They were shed for one who had gone astray,
 Ere the Shepherd could bring him back."
"Lord, whence are Thy hands so rent and torn?"
"They are pierced tonight by many a thorn."

But all through the mountains, thunder riven,
 And up from the rocky steep,
There arose a cry to the gate of Heaven,
 "Rejoice! I have found My sheep!"
And the angels echoed around the throne,
"Rejoice, for the Lord brings back His own!"

"Amidst us our Beloved stands"

Charles Haddon Spurgeon (1834-1892)

Charles Haddon Spurgeon.

Charles Haddon Spurgeon was born at Kelvedon in Essex on June 19th, 1834. When he was ten months old, the family moved to Colchester. A large part of Charles' childhood was spent at Stambourne with his grand-parents, and it was while there that Richard Knill of the London Missionary Society made a remarkable prediction concerning him. Greatly taken to the ten-year-old boy and taking him upon his knee he said, "I feel a solemn presentiment that this child will preach the gospel to thousands and God will bless him to their souls". Charles Haddon Spurgeon was converted when he was fifteen and died at fifty-seven and in the course of the intervening years, he preached to multitudes the simple gospel that he himself had received and thousands of souls were saved under his ministry. Christ was ever central in his message. No matter what part of the Bible gave him his text, sooner or later he found his way to Christ. We listen to him during those years: "Sinner, it is not thy hold of Christ that saves thee—it is Christ; . . . it is not prayer, it is not faith, it is not our doings, it is not our feelings upon which we must trust, but upon Christ, and on Christ alone . . . Let me beseech thee, look only to Christ." "Look only to Christ"; that was the central message of the prince of preachers.

"Look only to Christ"—that was the message that brought salvation to his own dark and burdened heart on that never-to-be forgotten snowy Sunday morning, January 6th, 1850. As a boy he had read much of the Puritans. Sin had become a reality, an intolerable burden. God's majesty and his own sinfulness had become such that he confessed, "I could not have gone to Heaven with my sin unpardoned, even if I had the offer to do it". In recounting salvation's experience he said, "I resolved that in the town where I lived, I would visit every place of worship in order to find out the way of salvation . . . At last one snowy day, I could not go to the place I had determined to go to . . . I turned down a court and there was a primitive Methodist chapel. I wanted to know how I might be saved . . . Settling down, the service went on but no minister came. At last a very thin-looking man came into the pulpit and opened his Bible and read the words, 'Look unto Me and be ye saved, all the ends of the earth' (Isaiah 45:22). Just setting his eyes upon me as if he knew all my heart, he said, 'Young man, you are in trouble . . . You will never get out of it unless you look to Christ'. And then, lifting up his hands, he cried out . . . 'Look, look, look! It is only, look', said he. I saw at once the way of salvation . . . 'Look', what a charming word it seemed to me! Oh, I looked until I could almost have looked my eyes away; and in Heaven I will look still, in joy unutterable!" A simple tablet marks the spot in that little Methodist chapel in Artillery Street, Colchester where Charles Haddon Spurgeon looked to Christ and passed from death unto life.

In the same year, 1850, young Spurgeon, though only a few months saved, became greatly exercised regarding preaching the gospel to others. He wrote to his father: "How I long for the time when it may please God to make me, like you my father, a successful preacher of the gospel. Oh, that I might see one sinner constrained to come to Jesus". He started to preach when he was sixteen. A deep joy filled his heart when during his short pastorate at Waterbeach, a woman trusted the Saviour, "I felt like a diver" he said, "who had been down to the depths of the sea and brought up a rare pearl". That was only the beginning. God was to use him mightily.

At the age of nineteen, London called and young Spurgeon moved to wider service. London was now his new mission field and there the need was great. With deep humility of spirit he moved to New Park Street Baptist chapel and starting with a small congregation of about two hundred, he preached Christ to them. God was with him and ere long the chapel was filled to its full capacity of twelve hundred. The building was enlarged but proved inadequate. Then the Metropolitan Tabernacle, planned to seat five thousand, was built and opened in 1861, and there Spurgeon ministered faithfully and fruitfully for the next thirty-one years, and over all that period, there was scarcely a meeting when God did not bless in salvation. E. W. Bacon's testimony is this, "Never has London, or anywhere else, seen such a God-honouring, Christ-exalting, Spirit-filled, Bible-based, soul-winning ministry—a ministry consecrated to the dual task of bringing together the sinner and his Saviour, the saint and His Lord". And of Spurgeon himself he adds, "He came from the audience chamber of the Most High and stepped into that large human auditorium—the mouth piece of God.

Each week Spurgeon's messages were printed and widely circulated. They were translated and published in French, German, Dutch, Spanish and Italian and dispersed as widely as America and Australia. They were read in public and in private. They were read in hospitals, taken inside prisons and pondered over by sailors at sea, and were mighty unto the salvation of many.

The closing years of Spurgeon's fruitful life were weighed down by the sorrows of controversy. Through it all, he stood faithful to his Lord, but by the age of fifty-seven he was a worn-out man and on January 31st, 1892, he passed into the presence of his Lord whom he loved so dearly. As his body was laid to rest in West Norwood Cemetery, Archibald Brown pronounced a eulogy, beautiful and touching, yet so fitting to the memory of his dear departed friend:

"Beloved President, Faithful Pastor, Prince of Preachers, Brother Beloved, Dear Spurgeon—we bid thee not 'Farewell' but only for a little while 'Goodnight'. Thou shall rise soon at the first dawn of the Resurrection-day of the redeemed. Yet is the goodnight not ours to bid but thine; it is we who linger in the darkness; thou art in God's holy light. Our night shall soon be passed and with it all our weeping. Then with thine, our songs shall greet the morning of a day that knows no cloud nor close; for there is not night there.

"Hard worker in the field! thy toil is ended. Straight has been the furrow thou hast ploughed. No looking back has marked thy course. Harvests have followed thy patient sowing, and Heaven is already rich with thine in-gathered sheaves, and shall still be enriched through the years yet lying in eternity.

"Champion of God! thy battle, long and nobly fought is over; thy sword, which clave to thy hand, has dropped at last; a palm branch takes its place. No longer does the helmet press thy brow, oft weary with its surging thoughts of battle; a victor's wreath from the great Commander's hand has already proved thy full reward.

"Here for a little while, shall rest thy precious dust. Then shall thy Well-Beloved come; and at His voice thou shalt spring from the couch of earth, fashioned like unto His body, into glory. Then spirit, soul, and body shall magnify the Lord's redemption. Until then, beloved, sleep. We praise God for thee, and by the blood of the everlasting covenant, hope and expect to praise God with thee. Amen."

Spurgeon, like John the Baptist, had but one passion, one mission in life—to entreat others to look to Christ. As a boy of fifteen, he himself had looked, "I could almost have looked my eyes away; and in Heaven I will look still, in joy unutterable!" As a youth of eighteen, he wrote a poem and concluded with the lines, "One joy, all joys shall far excel—To see Thy face, Immanuel". As the prince of preachers, he untiringly entreated men and women to look to Christ. As his body lay in state in the Metropolitan Tabernacle and over sixty thousand people filed past to pay their last tribute, there upon his coffin lay the Bible, open at the text of Isaiah 45:22, "Look unto Me, and be ye saved". And today, as each time at the Lord's supper we sing the words of Spurgeon's dearly-loved hymn, "Amidst us our Beloved stands", it seems as if he is still saying to us, "Look only to Christ".

> *Amidst us our Beloved stands,*
> *And bids us view His piercèd hands;*
> *Points to His wounded feet and side,*
> *Blest emblems of the Crucified.*
>
> *If now with eyes defiled and dim,*
> *We see the signs but see not Him,*
> *Oh, may His love the scales displace,*
> *And bid us see Him face to face!*
>
> *Our former transports we recount,*
> *When with Him in the holy mount*
> *These cause our souls to thirst anew,*
> *His marred but lovely face to view.*

"We would see Jesus" (John 12:21). The quest of each longing heart down here will one day be fully realized. Then "they shall see His face" (Rev. 22:4)—His face, 'marred but lovely'!

"O, the deep, deep love of Jesus"

Samuel Trevor Francis (1834-1925)

Samuel Trevor Francis.

Samuel Trevor Francis was born in Cheshunt in Hertfordshire on November 19th, 1834. Like the boy Timothy, he was privileged to have a godly mother and a godly grandmother. He recalls the impressions of those early childhood days, of a grandmother who taught him his letters using the Sriptures as her textbook and of a mother whose prayer life he could never forget. "One of my earliest recollections" he recounts, "is going with my eldest brother into my mother's room and made to kneel with her, while she poured out her

230

soul in earnest supplication that her boys might grow up to be
God-fearing men", and God heard and abundantly answered that
mother's prayer.

Much of his early life was spent in the city of Hull. As a boy, he
demonstrated a propensity for writing poetry and compiled a volume
of poems in his own handwriting. His elder brother teased and
taunted the youthful poet about these compositions to the extent
that, in a fit of temper, the young Samuel Trevor tore them up and
sadly these have been forever lost. In his early years he also
demonstrated a love for music and at the age of nine joined himself to
the choir of Hull Parish Church. Two meetings which Samuel Trevor
attended as a youth in Hull city left lifelong impressions with him.
The first was when Mr. Akester, a chemist in the city, had asked him
"if he would like to see a man buried alive". He said that he would
and observed as Mr. Andrew Jukes baptized by immersion a believer
in the Lord Jesus Christ. The second was when he witnessed for the
first time a company of believers gather in simplicity to remember the
Lord Jesus.

In his late teens Samuel Trevor Francis moved to London with a
view to studying medicine but upon the death of his father twelve
months later, he relinquished all prospects of such a career. He then
took up work in London and, at that time, God through His Spirit
wrought a work of grace in his heart. His spiritual need became a
heavy burden to him and he spent hours in prayer crying to God for
mercy; but let S. T. Francis tell, in his own words, of that great
experience which brought peace to his troubled heart.

"I was on my way home from work and had to cross Hungerford
Bridge to the South of the Thames. It was a winter's night of wind and
rain and in the loneliness of that walk I cried to God to have mercy
upon me. Staying for a moment to look at the dark waters flowing
under the bridge, the temptation was whispered to me, 'Make an end
of all this misery'. I drew back from the evil thought, and suddenly a
message was borne into my very soul, 'You do believe on the Lord
Jesus Christ?' I at once answered, 'I do believe' and I put my whole
trust in Him as my Saviour. Instantly there came this reply, 'Then you
are saved!' and with a thrill of joy I ran across the bridge, burst
through the turnstile and pursued my way home, repeating the words
again and again, 'Then I am saved! then I am saved!'."

Soon after conversion, S. T. Francis identified himself with an
assembly of believers meeting at Kennington, and with such

companies he continued for all the years that followed. He engaged in the preaching of the gospel, both indoor and in the open air, and through his ministry many were converted to the Lord; the years that followed on the 1859 Revival were particularly fruitful. When Moody and Sankey visited London in 1873/74, Francis identified himself with that mission, at times deputizing for Mr. Sankey and leading the praise. In his labours, he travelled widely, visiting Canada, Australia, Palestine and North Africa. Seventy three years were spent devotedly in the service of the Lord and on December 28th, 1925, in the ninety-second year of his life, he passed away peacefully into the presence of his Lord.

The deep gratitude that flooded the soul of S. T. Francis on conversion's day ever remained with him through life and often found expression in poetry and in song:

> Let me sing—for the glory of heaven
> Like a sunbeam has swept o'er my heart;
> I would praise Thee for sins all forgiven,
> For Thy love, which shall never depart.
>
> A song of a sinner forgiven,
> And a song that is music to Thee;
> A song of a pilgrim to heaven,
> Yes, a song from a sinner like me!

The compositions coming from his pen were many and the subject matter diverse, but all stemmed from a deep devotion to his Lord and Saviour. Many of them first appeared in various papers and magazines and at the close of life, the author collected some one hundred and fifty-one into one volume of *Select Poems*. While engaged in this work he was stricken by partial blindness, but through the kindness and help of friends the volume was published. In its preface, the author stated that the book was not written in the interest of any party or school of thought, but for all who "love the Lord Jesus Christ in sincerity and truth".

Several of the hymns of S. T. Francis have found a worthy place in the hymnals and within the hearts of the Lord's people. The words of his, "Adoring Jesus" ('Jesus, we remember Thee') is very often the language of redeemed hearts gathered at the Lord's supper on the first day of the week. Its companion hymn ('Gracious God, we worship Thee'), in adoration of the Father, is perhaps less well known. In both of these adoration hymns, a recurring phrase is found which gives emphasis to the hymn's great central theme. His advent hymn, "I am waiting for the dawning" is another favourite; its language is truly that of an anticipating and expectant heart awaiting the coming again of the Lord Jesus.

The love of Christ was, however, the writer's grandest theme of all; in its atmosphere he loved to dwell, bathing in the warmth of its sunshine and drinking deeply of its stream. Then from his soul, thereby refreshed and satisfied, he poured forth the treasures of his lovely hymn:

> O, the deep, deep love of Jesus,
> Vast, unmeasured, boundless, free;
> Rolling as a mighty ocean
> In its fullness over me.
> Underneath me, all around me,
> Is the current of Thy love,
> Leading onward, leading homeward,
> To my glorious rest above.
>
> O, the deep, deep love of Jesus,
> None can tell the reason why
> He descended from His glory,
> Came to earth to bleed and die;
> I, a wrecked and ruined creature,
> Sinful, helpless, all defiled;
> But the love of God in Jesus
> Made me God's beloved child.
>
> O, the deep, deep love of Jesus,
> Spread His praise from shore to shore,
> How He loveth, ever loveth,
> Changeth never, never more;
> How He watches o'er His loved ones,
> Died to call them all His own,
> How for them He intercedeth,
> Watcheth o'er them from the Throne.

> O, the deep, deep love of Jesus,
> Love of every love the best,
> 'Tis an ocean vast of blessing,
> 'Tis a haven sweet of rest;
> Though polluted, sinful, wretched
> Yet He calleth me "His own!";
> He will lift me to the grandeur
> Of His everlasting Throne.

These are the first four verses of S. T. Francis' original hymn, entitled "Love of Jesus"; the complete hymn has eight verses in all.

S. T. Francis, like Samuel Rutherford discovered that the Saviour's love "hath neither brim nor bottom" and that "there are infinite plies to His love that the saints will never win to unfold". In these verses S. T. Francis has unfolded for us some of the plies of that Divine love:

—first, that it is **boundless** ("vast, unmeasured, boundless, free")
—second, that it is **causeless** ("none can tell the reason why")
—third, that it is **changeless** ("changeth never, never more") and
—fourth, that it is **matchless** ("love of every love the best").

The plies to the love of Christ, however, are infinite; each has its own distinctive beauty; all have been woven on Heaven's loom.

"Take my life"

Frances Ridley Havergal (1836-1879)

Francis Ridley Havergal.

Frances Ridley Havergal, the "sweet singer of England" was born at Astley in Worcestershire on December 14th, 1836, a few months before Princess Victoria acceded to the throne of England. Frances, daughter of Rev. W. H. Havergal, M.A., was the youngest of a family of four girls and two boys. As a child she was called "Fanny" but always liked to sign herself Frances. Her middle name "Ridley" stemmed from the godly Bishop Ridley martyred three centuries before.

235

Frances, as a child, was naturally bright, intelligent and extremely talented. She learned to read at the age of two, could read the Bible at four, and at seven started to write simple verse. She had a prodigious memory and by the age of twenty had committed to memory the four Gospels, all the Epistles, the Revelation, the Psalms and Isaiah's prophecy; the Minor Prophets she learned in later years. She was besides, an outstanding linguist, fluent in French, German and Italian and had a good working knowledge of Latin, Greek and Hebrew. As a pianist she was proficient in classical works; as a singer she was a talented contralto soloist, and as a composer met with the appraisal of many masters including the great Ferdinand Hiller of Cologne in Germany who said of her harmonies that he could give them almost unlimited praise. All this wealth of talent Frances placed at an early age on the altar of consecration, to be used henceforth only for her Lord.

Frances left on record the spiritual experiences of her early years. She tells us that as a young child she longed to be Christ's and at times even dared to whisper her inner heart's secret, "Oh, if God would but make me a Christian!". At eleven years of age, her mother died leaving with her words which thenceforth would become her life prayer, "Fanny dear, pray to God to prepare you for all He is preparing for you." The great spiritual crisis of conversion came when she passed her fourteenth birthday, "Then I committed my soul to the Saviour. I do not mean to say without any trembling or fear but I did...and earth and heaven seemed bright from the moment...I did trust the Lord Jesus".

When Frances was seventeen she was confirmed in Worcester Cathedral; that ceremony left with her deep and lasting impressions for it was then that the thought of "whose I am" burst upon her for the very first time. Her heart was touched by the words of solemn pronouncement, "Defend, oh Lord, this Thy child with Thy heavenly grace that she may continue Thine for ever...". "Thine for ever"—what a thought! She wept and her heart thrilled with earnest longing. On that selfsame day, July 17th, 1854, within the cathedral she penned the lines,

> Oh! "Thine for ever," what a blessed thing
> To be for ever His who died for me!
> My Saviour, all my life Thy praise I'll sing,
> Nor cease my song throughout eternity.

The months and years that followed brought an increasing desire for an unreserved surrender of herself to God. The year of 1873 was for her a year of crisis, a year of unsurpassed spiritual blessing. "It was on Sunday, December 2nd, 1873, I first saw the blessedness of true consecration . . . that there must be full surrender before there can be full blessedness . . . I was shown that 'the blood of Jesus Christ His Son cleanseth us from all sin', and then it was made plain to me that He who had cleansed me had power to keep me clean; so I just utterly yielded myself to Him and entirely trusted Him to keep me".

Frances was then in the Master's hand, a vessel sanctified and meet for Him to use. She wrote then as she could never write before and it was at that time that she penned many of her immortal hymns, "My strong belief is," she affirmed, "that if I am going to write to any good, a great deal of **living** must go to a very little **writing**". Her prose meditations and hymns were saturated with the living Word of God and permeated with the fragrance of her devotion to Christ. "I can never set myself to write. I believe my King suggests a thought and whispers me a line or two and then I look up and thank Him delightfully and go on with it. That is how the hymns and poems come". She wrote prayerfully, verse by verse and line by line, like a little child; "You know a child would look up at every sentence and say, 'And what shall I say next?' That is what I do".

> I look up to my Father, and know that I am heard,
>   And ask Him for the glowing thought, and for the fitting word.
> I look up to my Father, for I cannot write alone,
>   'Tis sweeter far to seek His strength, than lean upon my own.

Throughout her days, simply and sweetly, Frances sang the love of God and His way of salvation. Many precious compositions flowed from her consecrated pen. Some sixty or more of these have been preserved to us and among them are some that are exceedingly fragrant as:

> "I am trusting Thee, Lord Jesus"
> "I gave my life for thee"
> "Like a river glorious"
> "Master speak! Thy servant heareth"
> "Lord, speak to me"
> "Precious, precious blood of Jesus"
> "Take my life and let it be"
> "Thou art coming, O my Saviour"

Of all her compositions, Frances' own particular favourite was, "I am trusting Thee, Lord Jesus"; its simple words of personal testimony and faith were discovered in her little pocket Bible after her death. Her best-known hymn, however, and the one by which she is remembered today is her great consecration hymn:

> Take my life, and let it be
>   Consecrated, Lord, to Thee;
> Take my moments and my days,
>   Let them flow in ceaseless praise.
>
> Take my hands, and let them move
>   At the impulse of Thy love;
> Take my feet, and let them be
>   Swift and beautiful for Thee.
>
> Take my voice, and let me sing
>   Always, only, for my King;
> Take my lips, and let them be
>   Fill'd with messages from Thee.
>
> Take my silver and my gold—
>   Not a mite would I withhold;
> Take my intellect and use
>   Ev'ry power as Thou shalt choose.
>
> Take my will, and make it Thine—
>   It shall be no longer mine:
> Take my heart—it is Thine own;
>   It shall be Thy royal throne.
>
> Take my love; my Lord, I pour
>   At Thy feet its treasure-store;
> Take myself, and I will be
>   Ever, only **ALL** for Thee.

This great hymn was written on the night of February 4th, 1874, at Areley House, near to Stourport-on-Severn. Let Frances herself tell the story of its writing, "I went for a little visit of five days (to Areley House). There were ten persons in the house, some unconverted and long prayed for, some converted but not rejoicing Christians. He gave me the prayer, 'Lord, give me **all** in this house!' And He just did! Before I left the house every one had got a blessing. The last night of my visit . . . I was too happy to sleep and passed the most of the night in praise and renewal of my own consecration and these little couplets formed themselves and chimed in my heart one after another till they finished with, "*Ever*, **ONLY, ALL** for Thee!"

The six verses of this hymn consist of twelve couplets, each of which is a prayer of the heart, an offering to the Lord, and it seems probable that each of them was born out of some distinct incident in Frances' own personal experience. "Take my voice, and let me sing, always, only, for my King" may be traced to the occasion when she declined to sing the part of Jezebel in Mendelssohn's Elijah at the Kidderminster concert. The couplet, "Take my silver and my gold—not a mite would I withhold" is most likely associated with the occasion of her sending all her jewellery and ornaments to the Church Missionary Society, keeping only for daily wear a locket and a brooch which was a memorial to her parents; on that occasion she wrote to a friend, "I don't think I need tell you that I never packed a box with such pleasure".

The life span of Frances Ridley Havergal was just forty-two years; still, those years were full for God. Then on June 3rd, 1879, to use her own words, she took

> *The one grand step, beyond the stars to God*
> *Into the splendour, shadowless and broad,*
> *Into the everlasting joy and light.*

While today, beyond the stars and within the gate of Heaven, Frances walks with God and sings as never before, still on earth she continues to speak through her writings—the fragrance and the fruit of a life consecrated wholly to God.

"Man of Sorrows!"

Philipp Bliss (1838-1876)

Philipp Bliss.

Philipp* Bliss was one of a band of spiritual noteworthies of the last century linked with the city of Chicago, U.S.A. That honoured band of evangelists, both preachers and singers, included names like D. L. Moody, Ira D. Sankey, D. W. Whittle, James McGranahan, George C. Stibbins and Charles H. Gabriel.

*Originally named Philipp Bliss; in hymnology known as Philip P. Bliss or P.P. Bliss; occasionally referred to as Philip Paul Bliss.

Philipp Bliss was born at Clearfield County, Pennsylvania, on July 9th, 1838, the third child in a family of five of Isaac and Lydia Bliss. Isaac Bliss was a humble and godly man; Philipp often referred to him and always with great affection—"the best man I ever knew; the Bible, the only book he ever read"; "he lived in continual communion with his Saviour, always happy, always trusting, always singing"—and having such a father, Philipp Bliss was truly blessed. Very early in life he put his trust in the Saviour and thereafter sought to live for His glory.

From early childhood Philipp had a great passion for music and his love for song increased with the passing of the years. He delighted to recount the occasion when, as a boy of ten, he heard a piano for the very first time. "A barefooted mountain lad had gone, as was his custom, to a little village with his basket of fresh vegetables which he peddled from door to door. One day, having sold his stock, he was on his way home when the sound of music was wafted to his ear through the open door of a house by the way; he paused; the music continued and drew him nearer and nearer until unconsciously he had entered the room where a lady was playing a piano accompaniment to the song she was singing. Entranced, he stood listening, his very soul lost in a sea of delight; such music he had never heard. Some movement of his attracted the lady's attention; she turned and seeing the boy, with a little scream of surprise cried out, 'What are you doing in my house? Get out of here with your great bare feet'."

At the early age of eleven Philipp was sent away from home to earn a living, first as a farm-hand and then as a labourer in a lumber camp. He was a wage earner for the family and in the winter months augmented his meagre earnings by teaching school. His marriage to Lucy Young took place ere he had reached his twenty-first birthday, and in the first years of their life together, Philipp worked on the farm of his father-in-law and taught music in the evenings in Bradford County.

When Philipp was twenty-two he had the privilege of attending a Normal Academy of Music course in New York and thereby his musical interest was deepened. He became a professional music teacher and started to compose simple melodies for Sunday-school work. He then moved to Chicago city and there continued his writing of hymns and songs. In this work he was greatly helped by the musician, Dr. George F. Root. His compositions were of a high order and soon he was renowned as a successful and accomplished musician. A promising career in the world of music then stretched out before him; he was at that time in his mid-twenties.

In Chicago city Philipp Bliss met with D. L. Moody; this marked the beginning of an intimate and lasting friendship, and by it deep impressions were made on both lives. Philipp Bliss was a spiritual man; to do the will of God was his sole objective in life; his one consuming passion was the salvation of souls. He thereupon gave up completely the composition of earthly songs and in the year 1874 when popularity, reputation, income and prospects were increasing, he surrendered his "all" entirely to the Lord, and stepped out into full-time service. God honoured and abundantly rewarded that step of faith and many souls were saved as he, together with Major D. W. Whittle, visited various centres throughout America; never was he more happy than when bringing to hearts the precious truths of the gospel in song and with a full heart, moist eyes and shining face.

At the early age of thirty-eight, Bliss's service for God on earth was brought suddenly to a close. On December 30th, 1876, he and his wife were involved in a railway disaster at Ashtabula, Ohio. The train bound for Chicago, on which they were travelling in the midst of a snow storm, plunged from a collapsed bridge to the deep ravine and river beneath. The carriages caught fire. Bliss managed to escape but his wife was trapped. He turned back to her aid and perished in the disaster.

Ashtabula was the dark river that bare Philipp Bliss to the heavenly home of which he so often had sung. His homegoing was glorious but the loss to earth was tremendous. At a crowded memorial service in Chicago, the chairman recalled Bliss's last message and song in that city, "I don't know as I shall ever sing here again, but I want to sing this as the language of my heart":

> *I know not the hour when my Lord will come*
> *To take me away to His own blest home*
> *But I know that His presence will lighten the gloom,*
> *And that will be glory for me.*

Mr. Goodwin addressed the large gathering, "Dear friends, God makes no mistakes. He has made none in allowing this calamity which has gathered us here in sorrow, let us make no mistake in reasoning about it ... We can as easily reason the darkness out of a room, as the darkness out of God's dealings. We get rid of the gloom when we stop debate, open the shutters and let the light shine in—the light of God's Word. 'Precious in the sight of the LORD is the death of His saints' (Psa. 116:15). 'Blessed are the dead which die in the Lord' (Rev. 14:13)".

Philipp Bliss composed many hymns; they were written to meet the need of the souls of men. "There is gospel enough in almost any one of them to lead a troubled soul to Christ; ... these songs were born in the closet and at the foot of the cross." The fervour of a gospel message or the poignancy of an illustration would at times so impress his mind as to suggest and set in motion the composition of a new hymn. On hearing Harry Moorehouse in the winter of 1869/70 preach for seven consecutive nights in Chicago on John 3:16, he was prompted to write, "Whosoever heareth! shout, shout the sound". His hymn "Almost persuaded" was composed as the result of hearing Mr. Brundage conclude an impressive gospel message with the words, "He who is almost persuaded is almost saved, but to be almost saved is to be entirely lost".

The gospel hymns of Philipp Bliss are great favourites and many are still sung nightly both on this side of the Atlantic and on the other. For a large number Bliss composed not only the words but as well the simple melodies to which the words are wedded and which have made his compositions so popular. The following are counted as among his best-known and best-loved:

> "Almost persuaded—now to believe"
> "Brightly beams our Father's mercy"
> "Free from the law, O happy condition!"
> "Ho! my comrades! see the signal"
> "I will sing of my Redeemer"
> "Man of sorrows! What a name"
> "Sing them over again to me"
> "The whole world was lost in the darkness of sin"
> "'Tis the promise of God"

"Man of Sorrows!" is one of Bliss's finest compositions; his picture of the Saviour therein is a lovely blend of suffering and glory.

> *Man of Sorrows! what a name*
> *For the Son of God who came*
> *Ruined sinners to reclaim!*
> *Hallelujah! what a Saviour!*

Bearing shame and scoffing rude,
  In my place condemned He stood;
Sealed my pardon with His blood:
  Hallelujah! what a Saviour!

Guilty, vile and helpless we;
  Spotless Lamb of God was He:
Full atonement—can it be?
  Hallelujah! what a Saviour!

Lifted up was He to die.
  "It is finished" was His cry;
Now in heaven exalted high:
  Hallelujah! what a Saviour!

When He comes, our glorious King,
  All His ransomed home to bring,
Then anew this song we'll sing:
  Hallelujah! what a Saviour!

Once a group of believers was travelling through the land of Israel by coach. "See, this is Benjamin country," remarked Linda, their Jewish guide, as they proceeded from Jerusalem towards Nablus (Shechem). On enquiry as to the meaning of Benjamin, Linda exulted to explain that at his birth his mother, Rachel, called him Benoni, meaning "son of sorrow", but his father, Jacob, called him Benjamin, meaning "son of my right hand". "Linda," said one of the group, "we have a lovely hymn concerning our Lord Jesus which expresses in song those truths of which you have been speaking". Then the company struck up the lines of Philipp Bliss's lovely hymn, "Man of Sorrows!". The heart of the Jewish guide was touched as she heard of One who had come in fulfilment of her Old Testament Scriptures, "a man of sorrows" (Isa. 53:3) and "the man of Thy right hand" (Psa. 80:17), in very truth the great antitype of Benjamin, the youngest son of Israel.

In Bliss's lovely hymn the matchless pathway of the Lord Jesus is traced afresh—His condescending grace in manhood, His spotless purity as "the Lamb of God", His perfect substitutionary work for guilty men upon the cross, His exaltation and coming kingdom glory. Each step of that pathway has its own distinctive glory; we pause to contemplate, then join in the words of the lovely refrain, "Hallelujah! what a Saviour!"

"Come, hear the gospel sound"

George West Frazer (1840-1896)

George West Frazer.

The birth of this widely known gospel hymn is very intimately connected with the conversion of its author, George West Frazer. Frazer, an Irishman, was led to Christ at the age of twenty, in the city of Dublin during the great revival of 1859/60. He had been born in the West of Ireland in the year 1840, the third son in the family of ten children of William Potter and Matilda Eleanor Frazer. His father was an Inspector of the Royal Irish Constabulary and had come to Ireland from Inverness in the north of Scotland.

The first step in George West Frazer's conversion was his spiritual awakening caused by the death of his younger brother. His older brother, William, had been converted to Christ and requested of

245

George that he would accompany him to the "Rotunda" in Dublin to hear Dr. H. Grattan Guinness preach the gospel. Large crowds were attending those meetings and there was much blessing. George consented to go and one evening the two brothers arrived at the "Rotunda"; they found the building full to overflowing and large numbers crowding the entrance. George determined, however, that at least he would see the preacher and so by climbing up an outside water-pipe he reached a second-storey window and from there he surveyed a sea of faces below. The preacher's voice came floating through the open window as he set to work upon his text for that meeting, "Yet there is room" (Luke 14:22). George West Frazer listened attentively as he heard the gospel preached with power; indeed, he heard the voice of God to his own soul and was troubled.

Fourteen days and fourteen nights of deep anxiety followed, during which he sought salvation but could not find it. At last he resolved to seek it no longer but have his 'fling' in the world. However, the contemplation of such a thought caused him to shudder, for he knew that in the end he would have to meet God. "If I must perish," he cried, "I am resolved to perish at His feet," and he cast himself at the Saviour's feet for mercy. The words of I Tim. 1:15 brought peace and assurance to his troubled heart, "This is a faithful saying and worthy of all acceptation that Christ Jesus came into the world to save sinners". Those words were sufficient to quell his fears and that night he slept like a little child.

Next morning George woke early to bear the news to his brother, but when about to leave he wondered, "What shall I tell him?"; the joy of the previous night had disappeared, his assurance of salvation gone. Then, in a moment, he recalled again the words of I Tim. 1:15, "This is a faithful saying and worthy of all acceptation that Christ Jesus came into the world to save sinners". That was the word that had first brought him peace and that word had not changed! George West Frazer in that moment perceived that the assurance of his salvation rested not upon his own feelings but upon the unchanging Word of God.

Frazer thereupon confessed Christ, first to his brother, then to his family and afterwards to a wider circle of friends. God acknowledged the faithfulness of his servant and blessing attended his witness. He was employed at that time as a clerk in Close's Bank in the city of Dublin and such was his godly testimony there that he commanded the respect and later the close friendship of his employing banker,

Mr. Farnham Close. He severed his links with the Church of Ireland and met simply with like-minded believers in assembly fellowship. That step was taken at no small cost for the Frazer family had had long-standing links with the Established Church and nine of his own cousins were at that time clergy in its ministry.

Times of close communion with God marked those early years in the city of Dublin. His days were happy but extremely busy. The preaching of the gospel, both indoor and in the open air, occupied more and more of his time until at last he decided to leave the bank and give all of his time to the work of the Lord. His early ministry centred around Dublin city but later he moved to England and lived in Cheltenham. In that Gloucestershire town he enjoyed and appreciated close fellowship with C. H. Mackintosh, the latter oft referring to him as his "son by adoption". E. E. Cornwall who knew and often heard Frazer in those days of his Cheltenham ministry wrote of, "his freshness of spirit and evident enjoyment of that whereof he spake. He delighted in the company of saints, and gave himself to their service: the meeting-room was to him a hallowed place".

Devotion to the Lord and obedience to His Word were ever the hallmarks of Mr. Frazer's service. However, at the early age of fifty-six, his days of service were complete and he entered into the presence of his Lord. His last testimony was both triumphant and blessed, "I grieve to leave my work for the Master . . . and all whom I love but it is infinitely more precious to me to be with Christ than all beside". It is indeed fitting that these lofty sentiments, expressed in lines from his own pen, should conclude the epitaph upon his tombstone in Cheltenham cemetery:

In loving memory of
GEORGE WEST FRAZER
Departed to be with Christ
January 24, 1896, Aged 56
"THOU REMAINEST" (Heb. 1:11)

His spirit now has winged its way
To those bright realms of cloudless day;
Then, mourner, cease to weep;
For better is it thus to be
From self, the world, and Satan free,
By Jesus put to sleep.

George West Frazer throughout life composed many hymns and these he published in three volumes—*Mid-Night Praises*, *Day-Dawn Praises*, and *The Day-Spring*. Though most of his hymns have now fallen into disuse, a few remain and are treasured. Perhaps, of all his compositions, none is more widely known or better loved than his gospel hymn:

> Come! hear the gospel sound—
>   "Yet there is room!"
> It tells to all around—
>   "Yet there is room!"
> Though guilty, now draw near,
> Though vile, you need not fear,
> With joy you now may hear—
> "Yet there is room!"
>
> God's love in Christ we see—
>   "Yet there is room!"
> Greater it could not be—
>   "Yet there is room!"
> His only Son He gave,
> He's righteous now to save
> All who on Him believe—
>   "Yet there is room!"
>
> "All things are ready: come!"
>   "Yet there is room!"
> Christ everything hath done—
>   "Yet there is room!"
> The work is now complete,
> "Before the mercy-seat,"
> A Saviour you shall meet—
>   "Yet there is room!"
>
> God's house is filling fast—
>   "Yet there is room!"
> Some soul will be the last—
>   "Yet there is room!"
> Yes, soon Salvation's day
> From you will pass away,
> Then grace no more will say—
>   "Yet there is room!"

Throughout this present dispensation God in grace is inviting sinners to Himself. In the gospel He announces to men and women the sufficiency of His provision to meet their every need and bids them to come. The gospel's mighty message once came to the heart of George West Frazer in the Spirit's power; the memories of its coming and that eventful night in the city of Dublin ever lingered in his heart—his late arrival, the crowded building, his place upon the window-sill, the preacher's fervour and most of all the arresting text and message of grace that reached his sinful heart. Ever afterward Frazer longed that others be enlightened and in this, his much-loved hymn, he clearly presents the truth of the glorious gospel, both in its blessed rich appeal and in its solemn warning note.

"O Love that wilt not let me go"

George Matheson (1842-1906)

George Matheson.

O Love that wilt not let me go,
I rest my weary soul in Thee;
I give Thee back the life I owe,
That in Thine ocean depths its flow
  May richer, fuller be.

O Light that followest all my way,
I yield my flickering torch to Thee;
My heart restores its borrowed ray,
That in Thy sunshine's blaze its day
  May brighter, fairer be.

O Joy that seekest me through pain,
I cannot close my heart to Thee;
I trace the rainbow through the rain,
And feel the promise is not vain
    That morn shall tearless be.

O Cross that liftest up my head,
I dare not ask to fly from Thee,
I lay in dust life's glory dead,
And from the ground there blossoms red
    Life that shall endless be.

George Matheson, the author of this beautiful hymn, was born on March 27th, 1842 in the city of Glasgow. His father was a successful merchant there and had earlier come with his wife from Sutherland in the north of Scotland. As a boy, George was afflicted with defective vision, possibly hereditary in its nature, and by the age of eighteen he was practically blind. He had, however, brilliant intellectual gifts and despite his serious handicap had a very distinguished career both at Glasgow Academy and Glasgow University. He finished university and the Seminary of the Church of Scotland with high honours and was licensed to preach in 1866.

Dr. Matheson's first experience in ministerial life was as an assistant for about two years to Dr. J. R. Macduff in Sandyford Church in Glasgow. In 1868, he was appointed to the parish of Innellan on the Firth of Clyde in Argyllshire and there he ministered faithfully for a period of eighteen years, while at the same time he proved his singular ability in theological, devotional and poetical contributions to literature. In 1886, he was called to the very large parish of St. Bernard's in the city of Edinburgh and there remained for thirteen years till ill health compelled his resignation in 1899. Dr. Matheson died at North Berwick, August 28th, 1906 and is buried in Glasgow.

Dr. Matheson never married but throughout his busy ministerial life his devoted sister Elizabeth was his constant companion. She aided him in every way possible, reading to him, writing for him and she herself learned the Greek, Latin and Hebrew in order to help him in his studies.

Dr. Matheson has gone down in history as one of Scotland's outstanding preachers, highly esteemed throughout the land and especially in the city of Edinburgh. In his ministries, both at Innellen and St. Bernard's, crowds flocked to hear him for there was a magnetism about the man that attracted people from all classes of society. The learned and the unlearned alike sat spellbound under his ministry for they discerned him to be not only a man of outstanding oratory and with unique intellectual powers but one who was in touch with the Living God. He poured his soul unreservedly into his message and it was said that George Matheson's sermons not only stirred his listeners to their core but thereafter vividly lived with them for the remainder of their lives. He preached before the Queen, Victoria, and she was so impressed by the blind preacher that she later presented to him a sculptured memorial of herself.

As a writer, Dr. Matheson contributed much. By his early thirties, he had already emerged in the literary world as no mean scholar and though many fine theological works from his pen appeared through the remaining years of his life, many consider that the finest book he ever wrote was his, *Studies of the Portrait of Christ*. In later life he concentrated more and more on devotional writings. These were unique in their character, widely read and greatly treasured; and such publications as, *Moments on the Mount, Searchings in the Silence, Words by the Wayside, Rests by the River, Voices of the Spirit* and *Leaves for Quiet Hours* ranked among the finest in the English language. His poetry in verse and song was published in one volume in 1890 (*Sacred Songs*) and therein are to be found compositions that will never die, as, "O Love that wilt not let me go", "Make me a captive, Lord, and then I shall be free", "Jesus, Fountain of my days" and "Gather us in, Thou Love that fillest all".

It is as a hymn-writer that Dr. Matheson is best remembered and none of his compositions is more loved than his "O Love that wilt not let me go". Dr. Matheson tells us that this hymn was the "inspiration of a moment" and he has left for us a very interesting account of its writing: "My hymn was composed in the manse of Innellan on the evening of the 6th June, 1882. I was, at that time, alone. It was the day of my sister's marriage and the rest of the family were staying overnight in Glasgow. Something had happened to me which was known only to myself, and which caused me the most severe mental suffering. The hymn was the fruit of that suffering. It was the quickest bit of work I ever did in my life. I had the impression rather of having it dictated to me by some inward voice than of working it out myself. I am quite sure that the whole work was completed in five minutes, and equally sure that it never received at my hands any retouching or correction. The Hymnal Committee of the Church of Scotland desired the change of one word. I had written originally, 'I climb the rainbow in the rain'. They objected to the word 'climb' and I put 'trace'." Though the author refers to his hymn as, "the fruit of suffering", it is interesting to note that he does not disclose to us the nature of that suffering, but simply says "it was known only to myself".

The hymn first appeared in the Church of Scotland magazine, *Life and Work* in 1883 and was entitled, "Jesus, All in All". Today it is found in many hymn books in almost every land. This beautiful and tender hymn has been complemented and further enriched by its fitting music, "St. Margaret", composed by the Scottish organist Albert L. Peace in 1884. Dr. Peace, having been requested by the Scottish Hymnal Committee that he write a tune for Matheson's text, read the hymn over and wrote the music straight off, adding "I will say that the ink of the first note was hardly dry when I had finished the tune".

This hymn, born in the very depths of the heart's experience, is at once an aspiration, a prayer, an affirmation. Matheson, in his hour of trial, when oppressed by disappointment, swamped by grief and attacked by doubt, lifted his eyes from the futile and temporal to the imperishable and eternal. Though things human and tangible had taken their flight and life's props been all removed, he perceived that there was something abiding, and that behind the shadows and through all the way there is ever "a Love that holds us", "a Light that follows us", "a Joy that seeks us" and "a Cross that lifts us". There had to be no withholding if he was to know life's best. In his *Moments on the Mount* he had prayed, "O God, Thou living God, let me fall into Thy hands; it is only in Thy hand that I can be perfectly safe. There is a pain with Thee which is not found without Thee, but it is the pain of love ...". George Matheson shrank not back; his soul rose to grasp the abiding, assuredly knowing that love, light and joy are inseparable from the cross of sacrifice and the tearless morn from the night of weeping.

"How great Thou art!"

Carl Boberg (1859-1940)

Carl Boberg.

O Lord my God! when I in awesome wonder
Consider all the works Thy hand hath made,
I see the stars, I hear the mighty thunder,
Thy pow'r throughout the universe displayed:

Then sings my soul, my Saviour God, to Thee,
How great Thou art! How great Thou art!

When through the woods and forest glades I wander,
And hear the birds sing sweetly in the trees;
When I look down from lofty mountain grandeur,
And hear the brook, and feel the gentle breeze:

And when I think that God, His Son not sparing,
Sent Him to die—I scarce can take it in ;
That on the Cross, my burden gladly bearing,
He bled and died, to take away my sin:

When Christ shall come with shout of acclamation
And take me home—what joy shall fill my heart!
Then shall I bow in humble adoration,
And there proclaim, 'My God, how great Thou art!'

"How great Thou art!" is a majestic, soul-stirring hymn begetting worship to Almighty God. Though written originally over one hundred years ago by Carl Boberg as a Swedish poem, "O store Gud" ("O great God"), the sequence of events by which it has so recently come to us in our English language is a fascinating story, involving many writers and translators, covering a period of over sixty years and taking us to many countries—to Sweden, to Estonia, to Russia, to Czechoslovakia, to Romania and to England. We are greatly indebted to Stuart K. Hine, not only for giving to us the English version of this hymn but also for the documentation of its fascinating story in booklet form—*The Story of 'How great Thou art!'*

The story of the hymn begins in Sweden in the year 1885. Carl Boberg, a young Swede, was then living in the town of Mönsterås on Sweden's south-east coast. He had been born there of humble parentage in 1859 and there he had been converted to God at the age of nineteen when, as "a sinner beyond measure" he found rest for his troubled heart in the promise of John 14:13, "Whatsoever ye shall ask in my Name, that will I do"—that Word of the Saviour had satisfied his heart. Boberg had reached the age of twenty-six and on a summer's evening was returning home from a meeting when he was overtaken by a violent thunderstorm. The lightning flashes and the thunder peals filled his heart with awe. The storm passed quickly and the rainbow appeared. On reaching his home, he surveyed the scene from his open window. It was an inspiring atmosphere—before him lay the Mönsterås inlet of the sea in perfect peace; across the inlet floated the song of the thrush from the distant woods, while the stillness of the evening was punctuated by the toll of the church bell. 'Twas then that Boberg composed "O store Gud" ("O Great God")—a lovely poem of nine verses.

This Swedish poem was translated twenty-two years later into the German, "Wie gross bist Du" ("How great Thou art!") by Manfred von Glehn, a resident of Estonia, and then from the German into the Russian by I. S. Prokhanoff, (known as the "Martin Luther of modern Russia"). Prokhanoff's version was greatly used of the Lord inside Russia but God was to send that message with accompanying blessing to yet wider spheres, and in His divine purpose Stuart K. Hine was instrumental in giving it to the English-speaking world. Mr. Hine first heard and learned it in the Russian when he and his wife were serving the Lord in Western Ukraine. There they used it much in their labours for the Lord and God honoured and blessed it, but the re-birth of the hymn in its English form awaited their arrival among the Carpathian mountain villages of Czechoslovakia and Romania.

Just as Carl Boberg was inspired by the beauty of the Swedish landscape after a summer thunderstorm, so Stuart K. Hine tells us that the first verse of the English version was inspired by a remarkable thunderstorm in a Carpathian mountain village in Czechoslovakia where he had been forced to take shelter for the night. The second stanza, "When through the woods and forest glades I wander" was penned in mountainous Bukovina in Romania, where among "the woods and forest glades" he one day heard a group of young Christians spontaneously burst forth into singing Prokhanoff's Russian version of "How great Thou art!".

The writing of the great third verse, "And when I think that God, His Son not sparing" is a thrilling story. Mr. Hine had been distributing gospels among the Carpathian mountain villagers. On arriving at one village, he found the Spirit of God already at work. Nineteen years earlier, through Divine providence, a Russian soldier had left behind him a Bible. However, no-one in the village could read and the Bible lay unopened through all those years. At length the wife of Dimitri learned to read and slowly she spelled out to her village neighbours the words of God's book. She had come to the story of the cross, and when Mr. Hine arrived, he found many hearts in that village melted and broken down by the love of God. What a story for those villagers! They had never heard it before. In their surrounding beautiful mountainous scenery they had seen God's handiwork but never before had they heard that "God so loved . . . that He gave His only begotten Son" and they "scarce could take it in" that Calvary had been divinely planned for them.

The hymn was completed many years later in England when Mr. and Mrs. Hine, forced to return to their homeland at the outbreak of World War II, were working among displaced Eastern Europeans. The incessant question in the hearts of those refugees, "When are we going home? When are we going home?" gave the stimulus to the composing of that lovely concluding verse.

Two optional verses, having their roots in Boberg's original poem, further extol the greatness of the heart of God. In today's world, their truth is very real, and so comforting for the child of God:

> *Oh, when I see ungrateful man defiling*
> *This bounteous earth, God's gifts so good and great;*
> *In foolish pride God's holy name reviling*
> *And yet, in grace, His wrath and judgment wait;*
>
> *When burdens press, and seem beyond endurance,*
> *Bowed down with grief, to Him I lift my face;*
> *And then in love He brings me sweet assurance:*
> *"My child! for thee sufficient is My grace".*

A simple two line melody befits the lovely words of this majestic hymn, born as a poem just over a century ago in south-east Sweden, hidden in obscurity for many years, put before the eyes of the world in its English form by Stuart K. Hine, and popularized during the 1950's by such elegant voices as James Caldwell of Central Africa and George Beverly Shea of America.

This is a great hymn for its theme is great. It speaks of God and God is great. "O LORD, my God, Thou art very great" (Psa. 104:1.) As Boberg gazed contemplatively on a tempest that was stilled he saw God there—sovereign, majestic, serene; and his heart, like David's, went on to ponder the great enigma, "When I consider Thy heavens, the work of Thy fingers, the moon and the stars which Thou hast ordained: What is man, that Thou art mindful of him?" (Psa. 8:3,4)—man, so proud and puny; man, so selfish and sinful—and yet God was mindful and God visited His creature in compassion and in

grace. The glory of God's creation had now been eclipsed by the glory
of His redemption. May the undivided praise be to **Him alone**.

> "Thou art worthy, O Lord, to receive glory and honour
> and power: for Thou hast created all things, and for Thy
> pleasure they are and were created" (Rev. 4:11).

> "Thou art worthy to take the book, and to open the seals
> thereof: for Thou wast slain, and hast redeemed us to God
> by Thy blood out of every kindred, and tongue, and
> people, and nation" (Rev. 5:9).

"O LORD, my God, Thou art very great". Within our hearts we feel
that He is too great for comprehension down here. Probably only
when we get "home" will we appreciate the greatness of our God.

> *Then shall I bow in humble adoration,*
> *And there proclaim; 'My God, how great Thou art!'*

Selected Bibliography

Bacon, Ernest W. *Spurgeon, Heir of the Puritans.* Baker Book House, Grand Rapids, Michigan 1967.

Barkley, John M. *Handbook to the Church Hymnary.* Oxford University Press, London 1979.

Beattie, David J. *The Romance of Sacred Song.* Marshall, Morgan and Scott, Ltd., London and Edinburgh 1931.

Beattie, David J. *Stories and Sketches of our Hymns and their Writers.* John Ritchie, Ltd., Kilmarnock, Scotland 1934.

Bonar, Andrew. *The Life of Robert Murray McCheyne.* (Reprint of 1944 edition). The Banner of Truth Trust, London 1962.

Bonar, Horatius. *Hymns of Faith and Hope.* James Nisbet and Co., London 1857.

Boreham, F.W. *A Late Lark Singing.* Epworth Press, London 1945.

Campbell, Duncan. *Hymns and Hymn Makers.* A. & C. Black, London 1903.

Clark, M. Guthrie. *Sing Them Again.* Henry E. Walter, Ltd., London 1955.

Colquhoun, Frank. *Hymns that live.* Hodder and Stoughton, London 1980.

Cornwall, E. E. *Songs of Pilgrimage and Glory.* (Part 1. and Part 2.) Central Bible Truth Depot, London.

C, A.R. (Cousin, Anne Ross) *Immanuel's Land and other pieces* James Nisbet and Co., London 1876.

Darby, J. N. *Spiritual Songs.* James Carter, London 1900

Deck, James G. *Hymns and Sacred Poems.* (Reprint of 1876 edition). Bible Truth Publishers.

Denny, Sir Edward, Bart. *Hymns and Poems.* G. Morrish, London 1889.

Duncan, Canon *Popular Hymns, Their Authors and Teaching.* Skeffington and Son, London 1910.

Francis, S. Trevor *Select Poems.* Pickering & Inglis Ltd., London.

Fountain, David *Isaac Watts remembered.* Gospel Standard Baptist Trust Ltd., Herts. 1974.

Gadsby, John *Memoirs of Hymn-Writers and Compilers.* John Gadsby, London 1882.

Gammie, Alexander *Preachers I have heard.* Pickering & Inglis Ltd., London.

Garland, Henry James *Henry Francis Lyte and the story of "Abide with me".* Torch Publishing Company Ltd., Manchester 1947

Gerhardt, Paul *Spiritual Songs.* (translated by John Kelly) Alexander Strahan, London 1867.

Gregory, Arthur E. *The Hymn-Book of the Modern Church.* Charles H. Kelly, London 1904.

Grierson, Janet *Frances Ridley Havergal.* The Havergal Society, Worcester 1979.

Havergal, M. V. G. *Memorials of Frances Ridley Havergal.* James Nisbet and Co., London 1880.

Hine, Stuart K. *The Story of "How great Thou art!"* Florentina Press, London 1958.

Holmes, Frank *Brother Indeed, The Life of Robert Cleaver Chapman.* Victory Press, London 1956.

Houghton, Elsie *Christian Hymn-writers.* Evangelical Press of Wales 1982.

Housman, Henry *John Ellerton, His Life and Writings on Hymnology.* S. P. C. K., London 1896.

Hughes, Glyn Tegai *Williams Pantycelyn.* University of Wales Press 1983.

Jackson, S. Trevena *Fanny Crosby Story.* (Reprint of 1915 edition) Baker Book House, Grand Rapids, Michigan 1981.

Jones, Francis Arthur *Famous Hymns and their Authors.* Hodder and Stoughton, London 1902.

Julian, John *A Dictionary of Hymnology.* Vol. 1, Vol. 2. (Reprint of 1907 edition) Dover Publications, Inc., New York 1957.

Keeler, W. T. *The Romantic Origin of Some Favourite Hymns.* Letchworth Printers Ltd. 1947.

Knapp, Christopher *Who Wrote our Hymns.* (Reprint of 1925 edition) Bible Truth Publishers, Illinois.

Langhorne, H. E. *Some Favourite Hymns.* Skeffington and Son, Ltd., London.

Lineham, Peter J. *The Significance of J.G. Deck.* Christian Brethren Research Fellowship, Wellington, N.Z. 1986.

Long, Edwin M. *Illustrated History of Hymns and their Authors* P. W. Ziegler and Co., Philadelphia, U.S.A. 1876.

Mable, Norman *Popular Hymns and their Writers*. Independent Press Ltd., London 1945.

Martin, Hugh *They Wrote Our Hymns*. S. C. M. Press Ltd., London 1961.

Morrison, Duncan *The Great Hymns of the Church*. Simpkin, Marshall, Hamilton, Kent & Co. Ltd., London 1890.

Osbeck, Kenneth W. *Singing with Understanding*. Kregel Publications, Grand Rapids, Michigan 1979.

Patrick, Millar *The Story of the Church's Song*. The Church of Scotland Committee on Publications, Edinburgh 1927.

Pickering, Hy. *Chief Men among the Brethren*. Pickering & Inglis, London 1918.

Pitman, Mrs. E. R. *Lady Hymn Writers*. T. Nelson and Sons, London 1892.

Pollock, John *Amazing Grace, John Newton's Story*. Hodder and Stoughton, London 1980.

Roach, Adrian *The Little Flock Hymn Book, Its History and Hymn Writers*. Present Truth Publishers, Morganville, N.J. 1974.

Routley, Erik *Hymns and the Faith*. John Murray, London 1955.

Sheppard, W. J. Limmer *Great Hymns and their Stories*. Lutterworth Press, London 1923.

Smellie, Alexander *Men of the Covenant*. (Reprint of 1903 edition) The Banner of Truth Trust 1960.

Stead, W. T. *Hymns that have Helped*. Doubleday, Page and Company, New York 1904.

Temple, Arthur *Hymns we Love* Lutterworth Press, London 1954.

Thomson, D. P. *Women of the Scottish Church*. Munroe and Scott, Perth 1975.

Thomson, Ronald W. *Who's Who of Hymn Writers*. Epworth Press, London 1967.

Turner, W. G. *John Nelson Darby*. (Reprint of 1901 edition) Chapter Two, London 1986.

Waudby, Fred C. *Immortal Music*. Victory Press, London 1932.

Whittle, D. W. *Memoir of P. P. Bliss*. F. E. Longley, London 1877.

Index of Authors

Index of Hymns (First Lines)

(Title hymns in bold type)

263